OPPOSING
VIEWPOINTS®
SERIES

MW01125448

Climate Justice and Greenwashing

Other Books of Related Interest

Opposing Viewpoints Series

America's Infrastructure and the Green Economy
The Politics of Climate
Renewable and Alternative Energy

At Issue Series

Environmental Racism and Classism
Pipelines and Politics
The Role of Science in Public Policy

Current Controversies Series

Climate Change and Biodiversity
Fossil Fuel Industries and the Green Economy
Sustainable Consumption

> "Congress shall make no law ... abridging the freedom of speech, or of the press."
>
> *First Amendment to the U.S. Constitution*

The basic foundation of our democracy is the First Amendment guarantee of freedom of expression. The Opposing Viewpoints series is dedicated to the concept of this basic freedom and the idea that it is more important to practice it than to enshrine it.

OPPOSING
VIEWPOINTS®
SERIES

Climate Justice and Greenwashing

Avery Elizabeth Hurt, Book Editor

GREENHAVEN
PUBLISHING

Published in 2025 by Greenhaven Publishing, LLC
2544 Clinton Street,
Buffalo NY 14224

First Edition

Articles in Greenhaven Publishing anthologies are often edited for length to meet page
requirements. In addition, original titles of these works are changed to clearly present
the main thesis and to explicitly indicate the author's opinion. Every effort is made to
ensure that Greenhaven Publishing accurately reflects the original intent of the authors.
Every effort has been made to trace the owners of the copyrighted material.

Cover image: Phonlamai Photo/Shutterstock.com

CataloginginPublication Data
Names: Hurt, Avery Elizabeth, editor.
Title: Climate justice and greenwashing / edited by Avery Elizabeth Hurt.
Description: First edition. | New York : Greenhaven Publishing, 2025. | Series:
Opposing viewpoints | Includes bibliographical references and index.
Identifiers: ISBN 9781534509856 (pbk.) | ISBN 9781534509863 (library bound)
Subjects: LCSH: Climate justice. | Environmental ethics. |
Greenwashing. | Corporations--Environmental aspects.
Classification: LCC GE220.C556 2025 | DDC 363.738'7452--dc23

Manufactured in the United States of America

Website: http://greenhavenpublishing.com

Contents

The Importance of Opposing Viewpoints   **11**

Introduction   **14**

Chapter 1: What Responsibility Do Nations Have for Climate Change?

Chapter Preface   **18**

1. Wealthy Nations Owe Poorer Ones for the
   Damage of Climate Change   **20**
   Bethany Tietjen

2. Rich Nations Balk at Paying for the Damage
   Caused by Climate Change   **25**
   Lauren Sommer

3. The Cooperation of All Countries Is Necessary
   to Prevent Biodiversity Loss and Climate Change   **32**
   Greg Asner

4. Foreign Investment Laws Stand in the Way of
   Climate Justice for Developing Countries   **37**
   Olabisi D. Akinkugbe

5. Financial Inclusion Can Help the Poor Build
   Resilience to Climate Shocks   **43**
   Sophie Sirtaine and Claudia McKay

6. Access to a Healthy Environment Is a Universal
   Human Right All Countries Must Honor   **50**
   Joel E. Correia

7. Global Climate Agreements Must Require
   Greater Action from Nations   **55**
   Lindsay Maizland

Periodical and Internet Sources Bibliography   **64**

Chapter 2: What Responsibility Do Corporations Have for Climate Change?

Chapter Preface   **67**

1. Ideology Can Eclipse Science When It Comes
   to Climate Change Policy   68
   Kerrie L. Unsworth, Sally V. Russell, and Matthew C. Davis

2. Big Oil, Rich Countries, and Carbon Billionaires
   Are Responsible for Climate Change—and Getting
   Away with It   74
   Oxfam America

3. Big Oil Must Be Held Accountable   79
   Patrick Parenteau and John Dernbach

4. Banning Financing for Fossil Fuel Projects in
   Africa Won't Solve Climate Change or Inequality   84
   Benjamin Attia and Morgan Bazilian

5. Capitalism Can and Must Evolve to Meet the
   Challenges of Climate Change   90
   Andrew J. Hoffman

Periodical and Internet Sources Bibliography   99

Chapter 3: What Role Should Social Justice Play in Decisions About Climate Change?

Chapter Preface   102

1. The Impacts of Climate Change Affect
   Marginalized Communities More   103
   Tahseen Jafry

2. Climate Change Is Setting Back Progress in
   Reducing Global Inequality   107
   Céline Guivarch, Nicolas Taconet, and Aurélie Méjean

3. Losses and Damage Can Be Lessened by
   Working with Vulnerable Communities   114
   Jon Barnett and Arghya Sinha Roy

4. Climate Justice and Social Justice Are Two Sides
   of the Same Coin   119
   Ghiwa Nakat

5. Gender Inequality and Climate Change
   Are Interconnected   123
   UN Women

6. Women and Gender-Diverse People Are Much
   More Likely to Die in Climate Disasters than Men   127
   Carla Pascoe Leahy

Periodical and Internet Sources Bibliography   132

Chapter 4: Do Corporations Often Engage in Greenwashing?

Chapter Preface   135

1. Greenwashing Doesn't Have to Be Overtly
   False to Be Deceptive   137
   Tom Lyon

2. Eco-Labels Must Be Standardized   143
   The British Standards Institution

3. Companies Use Deceitful Marketing Techniques
   to Make Consumers Think They're Green   149
   Christine Parker

4. Consumers Often Give Polluting Companies
   a Pass for Greenwashing   154
   Adam Austen Kay

5. Sustainability Reports Often Facilitate Greenwashing 159
   Hendri Yulius Wijaya and Kate Macdonald

Periodical and Internet Sources Bibliography   164

For Further Discussion   165
Organizations to Contact   167
Bibliography of Books   171
Index   173

The Importance of Opposing Viewpoints

Perhaps every generation experiences a period in time in which the populace seems especially polarized, starkly divided on the important issues of the day and gravitating toward the far ends of the political spectrum and away from a consensus-facilitating middle ground. The world that today's students are growing up in and that they will soon enter into as active and engaged citizens is deeply fragmented in just this way. Issues relating to terrorism, immigration, women's rights, minority rights, race relations, health care, taxation, wealth and poverty, the environment, policing, military intervention, the proper role of government—in some ways, perennial issues that are freshly and uniquely urgent and vital with each new generation—are currently roiling the world.

If we are to foster a knowledgeable, responsible, active, and engaged citizenry among today's youth, we must provide them with the intellectual, interpretive, and critical-thinking tools and experience necessary to make sense of the world around them and of the all-important debates and arguments that inform it. After all, the outcome of these debates will in large measure determine the future course, prospects, and outcomes of the world and its peoples, particularly its youth. If they are to become successful members of society and productive and informed citizens, students need to learn how to evaluate the strengths and weaknesses of someone else's arguments, how to sift fact from opinion and fallacy, and how to test the relative merits and validity of their own opinions against the known facts and the best possible available information. The landmark series Opposing Viewpoints has been providing students with just such critical-thinking skills and exposure to the debates surrounding society's most urgent contemporary issues for many years, and it continues to serve this essential role with undiminished commitment, care, and rigor.

The key to the series's success in achieving its goal of sharpening students' critical-thinking and analytic skills resides in its title—

Opposing Viewpoints. In every intriguing, compelling, and engaging volume of this series, readers are presented with the widest possible spectrum of distinct viewpoints, expert opinions, and informed argumentation and commentary, supplied by some of today's leading academics, thinkers, analysts, politicians, policy makers, economists, activists, change agents, and advocates. Every opinion and argument anthologized here is presented objectively and accorded respect. There is no editorializing in any introductory text or in the arrangement and order of the pieces. No piece is included as a "straw man," an easy ideological target for cheap point-scoring. As wide and inclusive a range of viewpoints as possible is offered, with no privileging of one particular political ideology or cultural perspective over another. It is left to each individual reader to evaluate the relative merits of each argument— as they see it, and with the use of ever-growing critical-thinking skills—and grapple with their own assumptions, beliefs, and perspectives to determine how convincing or successful any given argument is and how the reader's own stance on the issue may be modified or altered in response to it.

This process is facilitated and supported by volume, chapter, and selection introductions that provide readers with the essential context they need to begin engaging with the spotlighted issues, with the debates surrounding them, and with their own perhaps shifting or nascent opinions on them. In addition, guided reading and discussion questions encourage readers to determine the authors' point of view and purpose, interrogate and analyze the various arguments and their rhetoric and structure, evaluate the arguments' strengths and weaknesses, test their claims against available facts and evidence, judge the validity of the reasoning, and bring into clearer, sharper focus the reader's own beliefs and conclusions and how they may differ from or align with those in the collection or those of their classmates.

Research has shown that reading comprehension skills improve dramatically when students are provided with compelling, intriguing, and relevant "discussable" texts. The subject matter of these collections could not be more compelling, intriguing, or urgently relevant to today's students and the world they are poised to inherit. The anthologized articles and the reading and discussion questions that are included with them also provide the basis for stimulating, lively, and passionate classroom debates. Students who are compelled to anticipate objections to their own argument and identify the flaws in those of an opponent read more carefully, think more critically, and steep themselves in relevant context, facts, and information more thoroughly. In short, using discussable text of the kind provided by every single volume in the Opposing Viewpoints series encourages close reading, facilitates reading comprehension, fosters research, strengthens critical thinking, and greatly enlivens and energizes classroom discussion and participation. The entire learning process is deepened, extended, and strengthened.

For all of these reasons, Opposing Viewpoints continues to be exactly the right resource at exactly the right time—when we most need to provide readers with the critical-thinking tools and skills that will not only serve them well in school but also in their careers and their daily lives as decision-making family members, community members, and citizens. This series encourages respectful engagement with and analysis of opposing viewpoints and fosters a resulting increase in the strength and rigor of one's own opinions and stances. As such, it helps make readers "future ready," and that readiness will pay rich dividends for the readers themselves, for the citizenry, for our society, and for the world at large.

Introduction

> *"The people in power can continue to live in their bubble filled with their fantasies, like eternal growth on a finite planet and technological solutions that will suddenly appear seemingly out of nowhere and will erase all of these crises just like that. All this while the world is literally burning, on fire, and while the people living on the front lines are still bearing the brunt of the climate crisis."*
>
> *-Greta Thunberg, Swedish climate activist*

In a 2022 resolution, the United Nations General Assembly declared that a healthy environment is a human right. Upon the passage of the resolution, Inger Andersen, executive director of the UN Environment Programme, said, "This resolution sends a message that nobody can take nature, clean air, and water, or a stable climate away from us—at least, not without a fight."

Yet that is exactly what is happening, especially to people who do not have the resources to fight. Poor nations and poor and marginalized communities are suffering far more than everyone else from the effects of climate change. Yet these are the people who have contributed the least to global warming. The term "climate justice" refers to the attempt to keep these vulnerable populations in mind when making decisions and implementing policies related to climate change. This means examining what rights people have, such as asking the question, "Is a healthy environment a human right?" It means asking who is actually responsible for climate change, and what duty those most responsible have to those most harmed.

Those are the kinds of questions the authors in this volume explore. In the first chapter, the writers address the question from the perspective of nations. What do rich nations, which historically have been the highest carbon-emitters, owe to smaller, less developed nations? Should they help pay for cleanup after natural disasters caused by climate change? Should they pay reparations? If we determine that they do owe reparations, how do we figure out how much they owe? And does paying reparations amount to admitting guilt, a step that could come back to harm rich nations later in lawsuits?

Chapter 2 asks a similar question, but in this chapter the focus is not on nations but on corporations. Big oil companies have not only contributed to global warming, they also have deceived the public about the effects of climate change as well as their role in it. The writers in this chapter ask what responsibilities these companies (and other companies who have contributed to the problem) have for addressing the climate crisis.

The third chapter looks at the effects of climate change not on poor nations specifically, but on poor and marginalized populations within countries, even within rich countries. The authors in this chapter examine the effects of climate change not just on poor communities and racial minorities, but on women—who in many countries do the majority of the agricultural work—and on young people, who will, after all, bear greater hardships from climate change for a longer time than older people.

The final chapter asks if corporations are really doing what they say they're doing to address climate change. This chapter deals with "greenwashing," the practice of companies deceiving the public about efforts to make their products and practices more environmentally friendly. Which companies do it? How is it done? And what can be done to prevent the public from being deceived?

The science of climate change is as settled as science ever can be. However, questions of how to address the problem—and address it fairly—are still very much open. In *Opposing Viewpoints: Climate Justice and Greenwashing* the authors take on some of the thorniest questions facing us today. These are ideas that we need to be thinking about, because there's not much time left to act.

OPPOSING
VIEWPOINTS®
SERIES

CHAPTER 1

What Responsibility Do Nations Have for Climate Change?

Chapter Preface

Climate justice would mean—among other things—that those most responsible for the problem bear more of the burden. However, this is not how things are playing out. Rich countries are clearly the greatest emitters of greenhouse gases, by a large measure. But the effects of climate change are hitting poor and developing nations much harder. Yet figuring out who is to blame and what taking responsibility would look like is a more complex question than it might at first seem.

The authors in this chapter look at the issue from a variety of perspectives. In the first viewpoint, the author covers the concept of "loss and damage" as it applies to the harm climate change has had on developing countries. But calculating a fair price for restitution is one thing; getting high-emitting nations to pay is quite another. In the second viewpoint, the author looks at the reasons rich nations are hesitant to pay up, even after agreeing to do so.

Then in the third viewpoint, the discussion shifts from issues of paying reparations to the question of how to address the problem of climate change itself. This author argues that despite the inequities involved, any solution must necessarily require cooperation among all nations, rich and poor alike.

Not so fast, says the author of the fourth viewpoint. While cooperation *is* necessary to solve the problem and poor nations must have a voice in decision making, pushing developing nations to reach net-zero carbon emissions before they even have widespread electricity is too much to ask. Foreign investment laws make it so this transition would also cause more harm to developing countries than developed ones. The transition to renewable energy must be practical and equitable, and rich countries should bear more of the burden, he argues.

The fifth viewpoint considers what financial inclusion would look like in the era of climate change. In the sixth viewpoint in this chapter, the author argues that a healthy, sustainable environment is a human right, as established by the United Nations, and as such it is every country's responsibility to support this goal. Finally, the last viewpoint looks at attempts to establish international climate agreements—both successful and unsuccessful.

> *"The conversation on loss and damage is inherently about equity. It evokes the question: Why should countries that have done little to cause global warming be responsible for the damage resulting from the emissions of wealthy countries?"*

Wealthy Nations Owe Poorer Ones for the Damage of Climate Change

Bethany Tietjen

In this viewpoint Bethany Tietjen explains what the phrase "loss and damage" means in conversations about climate change and lays out the argument for why poorer countries that produce fewer greenhouse gas emissions should be compensated by wealthier countries. This has been a point of contention in many international conversations, including the 2022 UN Climate Change Conference, which was held in Egypt and is discussed in this viewpoint. Tietjen examines what a formal mechanism for loss and damage compensation might look like and the challenges countries face in reaching an agreement on this. Bethany Tietjen is a research fellow in climate policy at the Fletcher School at Tufts University.

As you read, consider the following questions:

1. How is "loss and damage" defined in this viewpoint?
2. What impacts have extreme rainfall had on Pakistan? What percent of global greenhouse gas emissions are they responsible for?
3. According to this viewpoint, why are developed countries reluctant to formalize a loss and damage mechanism?

You may be hearing the phrase "loss and damage" in the coming weeks as government leaders meet in Egypt for the 2022 UN Climate Change Conference.

It refers to the costs, both economic and physical, that developing countries are facing from climate change impacts. Many of the world's most climate-vulnerable countries have done little to cause climate change, yet they are experiencing extreme heat waves, floods, and other climate-related disasters. They want wealthier nations—historically the biggest sources of greenhouse gas emissions—to pay for the harm.

A powerful example is Pakistan, where extreme rainfall on the heels of a glacier-melting heat wave flooded nearly one-third of the country in the summer of 2022.

The flooding turned Pakistan's farm fields into miles-wide lakes that stranded communities for weeks. More than 1,700 people died, millions lost their homes and livelihoods, and more than 4 million acres of crops and orchards, as well as livestock, drowned or were damaged. This was followed by a surge in malaria cases as mosquitoes bred in the stagnant water.

Pakistan contributes only about 1 percent of the global greenhouse gas emissions driving climate change. But greenhouse gases don't stay within national borders—emissions anywhere affect the global climate. A warming climate intensifies rainfall, and studies suggest climate change may have increased Pakistan's rainfall intensity by as much as 50 percent.

The question of payments for loss and damage has been a long-standing point of negotiation at United Nations climate conferences, held nearly every year since 1995, but there has been little progress toward including a financial mechanism for loss and damage in international climate agreements.

Many developing countries are looking to this year's conference, COP27, as a crucial moment for making progress on establishing that formal mechanism.

Africa's Climate Conference

With Egypt hosting this year's UN climate conference, it's not surprising that loss and damage will take center stage.

Countries in Africa have some of the lowest national greenhouse gas emissions, and yet the continent is home to many of the world's most climate-vulnerable countries.

To deal with climate change, these countries—many of them among the world's poorest—will have to invest in adaptation measures, such as seawalls, climate-smart agriculture, and infrastructure that's more resilient to high heat and extreme storms. The UN Environment Program's Adaptation Gap Report, released Nov. 3, 2022, found that developing countries need five to 10 times more international adaptation finance than wealthier countries are providing.

When climate disasters strike, countries also need more financial help to cover relief efforts, infrastructure repairs and recovery. This is loss and damage.

Egypt is emphasizing the need for wealthy countries to make more progress on providing financial support for both adaptation and loss and damage.

Climate Injustice and Loss and Damage

The conversation on loss and damage is inherently about equity. It evokes the question: Why should countries that have done little to cause global warming be responsible for the damage resulting from the emissions of wealthy countries?

That also makes it contentious. Negotiators know that the idea of payments for loss and damage has the potential to lead to further discussions about financial compensation for historical injustices, such as slavery in the United States or colonial exploitation by European powers.

At COP26, held in 2021 in Glasgow, Scotland, negotiators made progress on some key issues, such as stronger emissions targets and pledges to double adaptation finance for developing countries. But COP26 was seen as a disappointment by advocates trying to establish a financial mechanism for wealthier nations to provide finance for loss and damage in developing countries.

What a Formal Mechanism Might Look Like

The lack of resolution at COP26, combined with Egypt's commitment to focus on financing for adaptation and loss and damage, means the issue will be on the table this year.

The nonprofit Center for Climate and Energy Solutions expects discussions to focus on institutional arrangements for the Santiago Network for Loss and Damage, which focuses on providing technical assistance to help developing countries minimize loss and damage; and on fine-tuning the Glasgow Dialogue, a formal process developed in 2021 to bring countries together to discuss funding for loss and damage.

The V20 group of finance ministers, representing 58 countries highly vulnerable to climate change, and the G-7 group of wealthy nations also reached an agreement in October 2022 on a financial mechanism called the Global Shield Against Climate Risks. The Global Shield is focused on providing risk insurance and rapid financial assistance to countries after disasters, but it's unclear how it will fit into the international discussions. Some groups have raised concerns that relying on insurance systems can overlook the poorest people and distract from the larger discussion of establishing a dedicated fund for loss and damage.

Two elements of developed countries' reluctance to formalize a loss and damage mechanism involve how to determine which countries or communities are eligible for compensation and what the limitations of such a mechanism would be.

What would a threshold for loss and damage eligibility look like? Limiting countries or communities from receiving compensation for loss and damage based on their current emissions or gross domestic product could become a problematic and complicated process. Most experts recommend determining eligibility based on climate vulnerability, but this can also prove difficult.

How Will World Leaders Respond?

Over a decade ago, developed countries committed to provide US$100 billion per year to fund adaptation and mitigation in developing countries. But they have been slow to meet that commitment, and it does not cover the damages from the climate impacts the world is already seeing today.

Establishing a loss and damage mechanism is considered one avenue to provide recourse for global climate injustice. All eyes will be on Egypt on Nov. 6–18, 2022, to see how world leaders respond.

> *"Developing countries have lower emissions, but are still bearing the brunt of a hotter climate through more severe heat waves, floods, and droughts."*

Rich Nations Balk at Paying for the Damage Caused by Climate Change

Lauren Sommer

In this viewpoint, Lauren Sommer points out that despite the fact that an abundance of evidence suggests that rich nations are much higher producers of greenhouse gas emissions and poorer nations suffer disproportionately, rich nations are resisting paying developing nations for damage done by climate change. Not long after this viewpoint was written, wealthy nations agreed to contribute to a fund to offset some of the damage, but so far, the fund is empty. Rich nations are afraid of assigning liability out of fear of the financial and legal consequences it may have for them. Lauren Sommer is a climate reporter for NPR.

As you read, consider the following questions:

1. How are developing nations "bearing the brunt" of climate change?

2. Why are rich countries hesitant to agree to pay reparations?

3. How have recent scientific analyses increased the pressure on rich nations?

B arbados Prime Minister Mia Mottley wants richer countries to stop throwing garbage in her yard and then telling her to clean it up.

The garbage, in this case, is greenhouse gas emissions that fuel more extreme storms and hurricanes, causing widespread destruction which can cost billions of dollars. At the Glasgow climate negotiations, Mottley is leading a push for richer countries to compensate poorer ones for the "loss and damage" caused by climate change.

Their argument is this: developed countries, like the U.S and those in the European Union, are responsible for most of the heat-trapping emissions pumped into the atmosphere since the Industrial Revolution. Developing countries have lower emissions, but are still bearing the brunt of a hotter climate through more severe heat waves, floods, and droughts.

"It is unjust and it is immoral," Mottley said at the summit. "It is wrong."

To help compensate for that, developing countries are asking richer ones to contribute to a loss and damage fund. The money could offer payment for things that are irrevocably lost, like lives or the extinction of species. It could also help countries with the cost of rebuilding after storms, replacing damaged crops, or relocating entire communities at risk.

While loss and damage was discussed at the Paris climate talks in 2015, progress has been slow. Industrialized countries have been reluctant to commit funding, concerned it could lead to being legally liable for the impacts of climate change. At this year's climate talks, developing countries say it's a crucial part of climate justice.

"Providing finance for loss and damage is the very least that wealthy countries can and should do," says Raeed Ali, a climate activist from Fiji and part of the Loss and Damage Youth Coalition. "But to do this, they will have to acknowledge that they are responsible for this. And I think that is something they are not willing to do."

Few Resources to Recover from Disasters

For countries with where much of the population lives in poverty, extreme weather can be a devastating blow. Individuals have little savings to rebuild, while governments with few resources struggle to secure the millions of dollars needed to help communities recover.

"In Fiji, we are at the forefront of the climate crisis," Ali says. "So every single person knows about climate change because it's a daily reality for us."

Ali says while his grandparents only remember experiencing one category 5 cyclone in their lives, he's already seen three. And with rising sea levels threatening to make villages uninhabitable, a handful in Fiji have already been relocated, and more than 40 are slated to be moved, he said.

Some countries are being hit by back-to-back disasters. In 2015, the Caribbean island nation of Dominica was hit by tropical storm Erika, causing more than $400 million in damage, equal to 90 percent of the country's gross domestic product. Two years later, Hurricane Maria slammed the island, damaging 90 percent of the country's housing stock.

In the Gambia in West Africa, where the majority of people in rural areas depend on agriculture, crop failures can be catastrophic. Because the country's main river flows into the ocean, rising sea levels are pushing saltwater farther and farther upriver, making it harder to get freshwater.

"It's really affecting the farming communities," says Isatou Camara, a climate negotiator for the Gambia in West Africa. "Because of sea level rise, we have saltwater intruding into our river which is affecting farm production, especially rice farming which is usually done along the riverside."

Developed countries have promised $100 billion per year in "climate finance" to help poorer nations reduce their emissions through things like renewable energy and sustainable agriculture. They've yet to fully deliver on that goal, since each country determines its own contribution.

But many developing countries say that funding doesn't help with the climate impacts they're already experiencing, which is why a separate loss and damage fund is needed. In 2020, natural disasters caused $210 billion in damage worldwide.

Assigning Liability for Climate Change

At the 2015 Paris climate summit, countries signed an agreement recognizing the need to address loss and damage. But developed countries pushed to include language that specified it did not "provide a basis for any liability." They feared that admitting responsibility for their share of heat-trapping pollution would expose them to paying developing nations every time a disaster hit.

"It's always something developed countries have been very cautious about exactly because they don't want it to be a precedent for international courts," Maria Antonia Tigre, a fellow at Columbia University's Sabin Center for Climate Change Law. "They really do want to avoid that responsibility because it can be endless."

Recent advances in climate change science have upped the pressure. While many climate studies examine long-term trends, researchers at the World Weather Attribution initiative study whether climate change has amplified an extreme weather event in the weeks or months after it hits.

Hurricane Harvey, which released a deluge of rain on Houston in 2017, was made 15 percent more intense by climate change, they found. This past summer, the severe heat wave in the Pacific Northwest that caused dozens of deaths was virtually impossible without the added boost of human-caused greenhouse gas emissions.

"The fact that we are able to pinpoint the climate fingerprint in specific things that hurt us today, I think, is a very important

WHO ARE THE TOP GREENHOUSE GAS EMITTERS?

The top three GHG emitters—China, the United States, and India—contribute 42.6 percent of total emissions, while the bottom 100 countries only account for 2.9 percent.

It's interesting to note that while India ranks high among emitters, when you factor in population to look at per capita GHG emissions, the highly populated country ranks significantly lower than the other top 10 emitters.

Collectively, this group of nations account for over two-thirds of global GHG emissions. The world cannot successfully fight climate change without significant action from the top 10 emitters.

[...]

Many Top Emitters Are Reducing Their Emissions Per Capita

While the top 10 emitters in total increased their emissions by 56.6 percent since 1990, the United States, European Union, Russia, and Japan have since peaked their per capita emissions.

More recent data from the Global Carbon Project, which covers energy-related carbon dioxide emissions, shows that emission growth has slowed down globally from 2013 to 2019, increasing by an average of 0.8 percent per year, compared to an average of 1.7 percent since 1990. This slowing of growth happened even as the global economy grew during the same period and 21 countries are already proving that decoupling emissions from economic growth is possible. In 2020, global emissions decreased by 4.9 percent as a result of the COVID-19 pandemic, making it the largest drop in emissions since 1960 (first year of available data for this source). In 2021, however, emissions grew back quickly, reaching a 0.1 percent increase over 2019 values, showing that emissions are still on an upwards trend, illustrating the need for increased climate actions to see a decoupling of economic growth and carbon emissions.

"This Interactive Chart Shows Changes in the World's Top 10 Emitters" by Johannes Friedrich, Mengpin Ge, Andrew Pickens, and Leandro Vigna. World Resources Institute, March 2, 2023 element in the current loss and damage conversation," says Maarten van Aalst, director of the Red Cross Red Crescent Climate Centre and a scientist with the World Weather Attribution initiative. "It has changed the conversation over the past years."

Van Aalst is quick to point out that assigning blame is a complex question. While a storm's destruction is caused by its strength, it also occurs if the buildings and homes aren't built to handle storms. Some communities aren't designed to endure the kinds of events that occurred even before the effects of climate change started to be felt.

Still, court cases are underway around the world to establish liability for climate change, either seeking damages from governments or fossil fuel companies.

"The uncertainty of science was one of the main arguments that was always used by states to avoid responsibility," says Tigre. "And that's a bridge that's now crossed."

No Show of Funding for Loss and Damage

At the Glasgow summit, Scotland announced a major milestone for addressing loss and damage needs. It offered 2 million pounds in funding, the first of its kind.

"That is in the right direction," said Sonam Wangdi of Bhutan, who chairs a group of the 46 poorer countries at the talks. "It's going to be very clear that there should be separate funds for loss and damage, and it should not be mixed with all the other funds."

Still, other funding commitments haven't followed yet. While the U.S. has formally recognized the need to address loss and damage, a senior U.S. official says the country doesn't support creating a dedicated new fund.

Instead of waiting for voluntary offers, Barbados Prime Minister Mottley is proposing using 1 percent tax on sales revenues from fossil fuels, which she estimates could raise $70 billion per year. Some are simply hoping that countries invest in the United Nation's Santiago Network, which was set up in 2019 to handle loss and damage issues. But without enough staffing and funding, it exists mainly symbolically today.

Even if developed countries offer new support for a loss and damage fund, they could still be held liable for the impacts of climate change. At a press conference in Glasgow, the island nations of Tuvalu and Antigua and Barbuda announced they're forming a new commission to enable small island countries to seek compensation through international courts.

> *"Technology is the easier part of the challenge. Organizing human cooperation toward such a broad goal is much harder. But we believe the value of Earth's biodiversity is far higher than the cost and effort needed to save it."*

The Cooperation of All Countries Is Necessary to Prevent Biodiversity Loss and Climate Change

Greg Asner

In this viewpoint Greg Asner asserts that countries must work together to build on the 2015 Paris Agreement, which created global targets for reducing greenhouse gas emissions. Asner argues that even more important than trying to reduce greenhouse gas emissions is protecting biodiversity, which he asserts is the most logical and cost-effective way to reduce greenhouse gas emissions since many ecosystems capture and store carbon. He proposes a "Global Deal for Nature" which would protect a large amount of the land and water across the globe. This would require cooperation from all countries, however, since he is calling for such a large number of ecosystems to be protected and there is a significant connection between these

"To Solve Climate Change and Biodiversity Loss, We Need a Global Deal for Nature," by Greg Asner, The Conversation, April 19, 2019, https://theconversation.com/to-solve-climate-change-and-biodiversity-loss-we-need-a-global-deal-for-nature-115557. Licensed under CC BY-ND 4.0 International.

ecosystems. Greg Asner is director of the Center for Global Discovery and Conservation Science and a professor at Arizona State University.

As you read, consider the following questions:

1. What percent of Earth's surface should be immediately protected to prevent biodiversity loss, according to Asner and his colleagues?
2. What are "ecoregions"?
3. What are the challenges to a Global Deal for Nature?

Earth's cornucopia of life has evolved over 550 million years. Along the way, five mass extinction events have caused serious setbacks to life on our planet. The fifth, which was caused by a gargantuan meteorite impact along Mexico's Yucatan coast, changed Earth's climate, took out the dinosaurs, and altered the course of biological evolution.

Today nature is suffering accelerating losses so great that many scientists say a sixth mass extinction is underway. Unlike past mass extinctions, this event is driven by human actions that are dismantling and disrupting natural ecosystems and changing Earth's climate.

My research focuses on ecosystems and climate change from regional to global scales. In a new study titled "A Global Deal for Nature," led by conservation biologist and strategist Eric Dinerstein, 17 colleagues and I lay out a road map for simultaneously averting a sixth mass extinction and reducing climate change.

We chart a course for immediately protecting at least 30 percent of Earth's surface to put the brakes on rapid biodiversity loss, and then add another 20 percent comprising ecosystems that can suck disproportionately large amounts of carbon out of the atmosphere. In our view, biodiversity loss and climate change must be addressed as one interconnected problem with linked solutions.

Let's Make a Deal

Our Global Deal for Nature is based on a map of about a thousand "ecoregions" on land and sea, which we delineated based on an internationally growing body of research. Each of them contains a unique ensemble of species and ecosystems, and they play complementary roles in curbing climate change.

Natural ecosystems are like mutual funds in an otherwise volatile stock market. They contain self-regulating webs of organisms that interact. For example, tropical forests contain a kaleidoscope of tree species that are packed together, maximizing carbon storage in wood and soils.

Forests can weather natural disasters and catastrophic disease outbreaks because they are diverse portfolios of biological responses, self-managed by and among co-existing species. It's hard to crash them if they are left alone to do their thing.

Man-made ecosystems are poor substitutes for their natural counterparts. For example, tree plantations are not forest ecosystems—they are crops of trees that store far less carbon than natural forests, and require much more upkeep. Plantations are also ghost towns compared to the complex biodiversity found in natural forests.

Another important feature of natural ecosystems is that they are connected and influence one another. Consider coral reefs, which are central to the Global Deal for Nature because they store carbon and are hotspots for biodiversity. But that's not their only value: They also protect coasts from storm surge, supporting inland mangroves and coastal grasslands that are mega-storage vaults for carbon and homes for large numbers of species. If one ecosystem is lost, risk to the others rises dramatically. Connectivity matters.

The idea of conserving large swaths of the planet to preserve biodiversity is not new. Many distinguished experts have endorsed the idea of setting aside half the surface of Earth to protect biodiversity. The Global Deal for Nature greatly advances this idea by specifying the amounts, places, and types of protections needed to get this effort moving in the right direction.

Building on the Paris Agreement

We designed our study to serve as guidance that governments can use in a planning process, similar to the climate change negotiations that led to the 2015 Paris Agreement. The Paris accord, which 197 nations have signed, sets global targets for cutting greenhouse gas emissions, provides a model for financial assistance to low-income countries and supports local and grassroots efforts worldwide.

But the Paris Agreement does not safeguard the diversity of life on Earth. Without a companion plan, we will lose the wealth of species that have taken millions of years to evolve and accumulate.

In fact, my colleagues and I believe the Paris Agreement cannot be met without simultaneously saving biodiversity. Here's why: The most logical and cost-effective way to curb greenhouse gas emissions and remove gases from the atmosphere is by storing carbon in natural ecosystems.

Forests, grasslands, peatlands, mangroves, and a few other types of ecosystems pull the most carbon from the air per acre of land. Protecting and expanding their range is far more scalable and far less expensive than engineering the climate to slow the pace of warming. And there is no time to lose.

Worth the Cost

What would it take to put a Global Deal for Nature into action? Land and marine protection costs money: Our plan would require a budget of some US$100 billion per year. This may sound like a lot, but for comparison, Silicon Valley companies earned nearly $60 billion in 2017 just from selling apps. And the distributed cost is well within international reach. Today, however, our global society is spending less than a 10th of that amount to save Earth's biodiversity.

Nations will also need new technology to assess and monitor progress and put biodiversity-saving actions to the test. Some ingredients needed for a global biodiversity monitoring system are now deployed, such as basic satellites that describe the general locations of forests and reefs. Others are only up and running at regional scales, such as on-the-ground tracking systems to detect animals and the people who poach them, and airborne biodiversity and carbon-mapping technologies.

But key components are still missing at the global scale, including technology that can analyze target ecosystems and species from Earth orbit, on high-flying aircraft and in the field to generate real-time knowledge about the changing state of life on our planet. The good news is that this type of technology exists, and could be rapidly scaled up to create the first global nature monitoring program.

Technology is the easier part of the challenge. Organizing human cooperation toward such a broad goal is much harder. But we believe the value of Earth's biodiversity is far higher than the cost and effort needed to save it.

> *"The design of the global transition from fossil fuels to net-zero emissions must account for the economic differences between countries and allow for multiple pathways."*

Foreign Investment Laws Stand in the Way of Climate Justice for Developing Countries

Olabisi D. Akinkugbe

In this viewpoint Olabisi D. Akinkugbe argues that climate change policies calling on all countries to make the shift from fossil fuels to renewable energy sources do not take into account that this is much more difficult for developing countries who would likely suffer an economic blow as a result. These policies do not acknowledge the economic imbalances between countries or the fact that foreign investment law would cause developing countries to be penalized if they make this shift. This is because certain legal protections are in place to protect foreign investors—such as fossil fuel companies— and developing countries risk facing expensive penalties if they pull out of these agreements. These issues must be addressed to ensure that climate justice is part of the transition to clean energy. Olabisi D. Akinkugbe is an associate professor and the Viscount Bennett Professor of Law at the Schulich School of Law, Dalhousie University in Nova Scotia, Canada.

"Low Emissions and Economic Survival—Countries in the Global South Aren't Getting a Fair Deal," by Olabisi D. Akinkugbe, The Conversation, November 29, 2023, https://theconversation.com/low-emissions-and-economic-survival-countries-in-the-global-south-arent-getting-a-fair-deal-217636. Licensed under CC BY-ND 4.0 International.

As you read, consider the following questions:

1. How does the United Nations Development Programme define climate justice?
2. According to this viewpoint, how do legal instruments protect foreign investors?
3. What four reasons does Akinkugbe offer for why climate change law and foreign investment law are at odds?

In 2015, more than 140 countries signed up to the goal of achieving net-zero emissions by 2050. For countries in the global south this is a huge task. On the one hand they have committed to low emissions. On the other their economic survival depends on using resources that produce high emissions. International economic law scholar Olabisi D. Akinkugbe unpacks the issue of climate justice, and how climate laws and foreign investment laws fit into the picture.

Climate change policies are designed to reduce greenhouse gas emissions (which mainly come from the use of fossil fuels) and shift socio-economic activities towards the use of renewable energies. But, unless these changes are made in a manner that considers historical responsibility for the economic imbalances between countries, they risk crippling the economies of the global south.

That's why institutions such as the United Nations Development Programme have called for climate justice, which means:

> putting equity and human rights at the core of decision making and action on climate change. The concept has been widely used to refer to the unequal historical responsibility that countries and communities bear in relation to the climate crisis.

A climate justice approach to climate change would consider that developing countries did not contribute to climate change as much as developed countries but bear a disproportionate burden of the impact of climate change.

Yet, as we detail in a recent paper, a combination of legal frameworks for climate change and foreign direct investment is making the situation worse for developing countries. These laws inform the debate on climate change.

THE 7 BIGGEST POLLUTERS BY INDUSTRY IN 2022

Here's are the top seven polluters by industry and their GHG emissions per year:

1. Energy (Electricity and Heating): 15.83 billion tons
2. Transport: 8.43 billion tons
3. Manufacturing and construction: 6.3 billion tons
4. Agriculture: 5.79 billion tons
5. Food retail: 3.1 billion tons
6. Fashion: 2.1 billion tons
7. Technology: 1.02 billion tons

The energy, transport, and manufacturing/construction industries make up the top three positions, respectively, and have a combined output of 30.56 billion tons of GHG yearly.

Despite the advancements and usage of renewable energy technology, fossil fuels are still the dominant source of energy and fuel. Energy is still by far the industry that produces the most pollution, at a rate of more than 15 billion tons due to its dependency on coal, oil, and gas.

Although electric vehicles were purchased in record numbers the last year, petrol vehicles are still the prominent transportation method, accounting for 74.5 percent of the Transport Industries' CO_2 emissions.

Shockingly, manufacturing and construction is responsible for 50 percent of all natural resource extraction worldwide. It's consumption accounts for one-sixth of global fresh water, one-quarter of wood, and one-quarter of global waste. The industry's practices need to be more sustainable, especially in regards to material sourcing and wastage.

continued on next spread

The workings of the food industry—comprising agriculture and food retail—means that they follow in the rankings (fourth and fifth) with a combined total of 8.89 billion tons.

The retail industry—food retail, fashion and technology—make up positions five, six and seven, respectively, with a combined amount of 6.22 billion tons.

[...]

Countries around the world have declared a climate emergency, plastic pollution is at an all-time high, we've seen the hottest years on record, and more animals have reached extinction. Ultimately, we've seen the impact of our consumerism skyrocket to new levels—which is reflected by this year's industry rankings.

Although this paints quite a bleak picture, it's not all bad. The past decade has also seen much of the world wake up to climate change—with some governments making active efforts to lower their emissions. We've seen an ever-growing use of renewable energy, climate strikes beyond belief, and the lowest use of coal in some countries since records began.

If a handful of industries adopt more sustainable practices, global emissions will decrease and we might be able to limit global warming to 1.5 degrees Celsius.

[...]

"The 7 Biggest Polluters by Industry in 2022, as Ranked in New Research" by Beth Howell. Environmental Protection, October 17, 2022.

What Are the Laws? How Are They Flawed?

International climate change law is a layered and complex set of principles, rules, regulations, and institutions.

The United Nations climate change regime is at the centre of the international action to address climate change. It does this by addressing mitigation and adaptation challenges. The regime includes the 1992 United Nations Framework Convention on Climate Change and the 2015 Paris Agreement. It also includes the Intergovernmental Panel on Climate Change (IPCC), and decisions of bodies like the Conference of Parties to the Convention ("COP") and the Conference of the Parties serving as the meeting of the Parties to the Paris Agreement.

The relationship between climate goals and international investment and trade has attracted more attention from scholars since the 2022 report of the Working Group III of the IPCC highlighted the incompatibility of climate goals and trade and investment regimes.

The Paris Agreement is the primary point of intersection between investment law and climate law. Among other goals, the agreement aspires to make finance flows consistent with low emissions pathways and climate resilient development.

In the study I argue that investment law and climate change law are at odds with the quest for climate justice. There are at least four reasons:

First, calls for ambitious and expedited transition to climate-friendly investments leave developing countries at a disadvantage in attracting new investments. Mobilising climate finance for a clean energy transition is expensive. As the finance is also primarily in the form of loans, it deepens the debt vulnerability of developing countries.

Second, treaty-based solutions don't adequately address the power imbalance in the investor-host state relationship. Investment treaties protect investors more than host states. Also, the investor-state dispute system has more consequences for developing countries. And there is disregard for public interest concerns in the award of damages to investors.

Third, embracing market-based solutions led by transnational corporations may reinforce climate injustice while barely reducing emissions. The profit-oriented nature of the investment approach exacerbates the existing debt challenges of developing countries.

Fourth, the risks of investor-state disputes, heavy damages, and compensation are generally skewed against developing countries. This affects their capacity to take climate action.

Legal instruments protect foreign investors. The legal protection of foreign direct investment under public international law is guaranteed by international investment agreements and bilateral investment treaties. In addition, multilateral investment treaties, such as the Energy Charter Treaty, and some free trade agreements also protect direct investment.

An investor can sue a host state for violations of treaties or investment agreements and get damages. Developing countries have been on the receiving end of punitive damages. This has led to calls for reform of the arbitration regime that applies to investors and states.

What Should Be Done?

The design of the global transition from fossil fuels to net-zero emissions must account for the economic differences between countries and allow for multiple pathways. This is particularly true for developing countries that must reorganise their economies to attract investments that reduce emissions and generate socioeconomic development, while addressing their debt exposures.

The misalignment of climate change law and international investment law deepens this challenge. This is because many African states depend on the extractive industry to sustain their economies. In addition, the global transition to renewable energy has wider ramifications to produce batteries, electric vehicles, and other renewable energy systems. All require mineral resources from the global south.

Green or climate-friendly investment places global south countries in an unequal position on the international energy chart.

Developing countries, therefore, face the dilemma of balancing fossil fuel extraction with climate-friendly investments. Increased demands for electric vehicles and renewable energy present opportunities for developing states. But many lack the capacity to capture parts of the supply chains of the new green economy.

The transition to net-zero emissions thus poses several problems: climate crisis, extreme poverty, and lack of access to energy.

> *"Climate disasters produce even more destruction through second- and third-order effects such as disease, malnutrition, displacement, conflict, and loss of livelihoods. "*

Financial Inclusion Can Help the Poor Build Resilience to Climate Shocks

Sophie Sirtaine and Claudia McKay

The authors of this viewpoint zoom in from the level of nation to the level of communities—even individuals—in analyzing who is suffering most from the effects of climate change. They also offer suggestions for how to mitigate these effects. They assert that financial inclusion is necessary for climate justice, meaning that money should not just be invested into cleaner energy, but into helping the developing countries that are suffering the impacts of climate change better adapt to growing climate risks. Sophie Sirtaine is the CEO of the Consultative Group to Assist the Poor (CGAP). Claudia McKay is the organization's lead on green and resilient outcomes. CGAP is a global organization working to advance the lives of people living in poverty, especially women, through financial inclusion.

"In an Era of Urgent Climate Risk, Does Financial Inclusion Matter?" by Sophie Sirtaine, Claudia McKay, Consultative Group to Assist the Poor (CGAP), June 2, 2022. Reproduced with permission.

As you read, consider the following questions:

1. What are the second- and third-order effects of climate change mentioned here?
2. Why do these effects harm the poor more?
3. Why do women and girls suffer more from the effects of climate change?

Poor people in developing countries contribute relatively little to carbon emissions, yet they suffer disproportionately from the impacts of climate change compared to people in wealthy countries. Rich economies are responsible for more than 92 percent of historic excess global emissions, and the richest 1 percent of people today produce more than double the emissions of the poorest 50 percent of humanity. But our focus in this essay note is not on who pollutes, but rather on who suffers from the impact of climate change. Indeed, we cannot just look at the climate hazard itself, nor just at its causes: as the Intergovernmental Panel on Climate Change has noted, we must also recognize who is being affected and the factors that make different people vulnerable.

Low-income communities are already being hit the hardest. Climate change manifests in first-order effects such as extreme heat and more intense and frequent weather-related natural disasters, leading to deaths, injuries, and the destruction of property. Major climate-related shocks like flooding, droughts, and storms result in 15 times higher death tolls (IPCC 2022) in highly vulnerable countries compared to the least vulnerable countries. Yet climate disasters produce even more destruction through second- and third-order effects such as disease, malnutrition, displacement, conflict, and loss of livelihoods. Because poor countries do not have adequate public health, institutions, and infrastructure to contain the damage, these second- and third-order effects further accentuate the gap in climate impacts between the rich and poor.

Women and girls suffer more than men and boys. Women make up 80 percent of people forcibly displaced by climate-related disasters in developing countries, and they are more likely to die as a result of natural disasters like droughts, floods, and storms (IPCC 2022). Women and girls also experience larger second- and third-order effects, including increased risks of gender-based violence, dropping out of school, and early child marriage. Similar inequalities beset other marginalized groups, including the very young, the elderly, ethnic and religious minorities, Indigenous people, and refugees (IPCC 2022).

While the poor suffer disproportionately, they have the smallest margins and least access to resilience strategies that can help them avoid, absorb, and adapt to shocks. Losses and damages are concentrated among the poorest vulnerable populations, as the intersection of inequality and poverty presents significant limits to adaptation responses (IPCC 2022). Moreover, any given loss affects poor and marginalized people far more because their livelihoods depend on fewer assets; their consumption is closer to subsistence levels; they cannot rely on savings to smooth the impacts; their health and education are at greater risk; and they may need more time to recover. Estimates of the impacts of climate change on the incomes of the poor found that, across 92 developing countries, the poorest 40 percent of the population experienced losses that were 70 percent greater than the losses of people with average wealth.

These stark inequities will surely grow worse as existing vulnerabilities and inequalities deteriorate further due to the effects of climate change (IPCC 2022). It is vital therefore that any development agenda, including financial inclusion, considers how poor and vulnerable households can build resilience and adapt to the climatic changes impacting their lives. Without taking into account the impact of climate change on the poor and vulnerable, no development initiative will be sustainable.

In November, the United Nations will convene COP 27 in Egypt. The COP's presence in Africa will highlight the necessity of focusing on adaptation alongside mitigation, and on including poor and vulnerable communities and countries in climate-change discussions. The conversation cannot just be about the poor and vulnerable: It must involve them to ensure it addresses their needs. That is not just the right thing to do, it is essential to ensure an inclusive and sustainable future for all.

Financial Inclusion Can Help the Poor Build Resilience to Climate Shocks

The current focus of the climate change debate, understandably, focuses on macro-level challenges, with a strong emphasis on mitigation. When it comes to financial services, the discussions largely focus on the greening of the financial sector and on ensuring financial stability during the transition to low-carbon economies. Climate Fintechs attracted $1.2 billion in investments last year, and they are developing innovative solutions around carbon offsetting, carbon accounting, and supply-chain analytics. These initiatives are essential.

Yet the challenge of climate cannot be solved by focusing on only one side of the equation. It is high time to also focus on the adaptation needed by the poor, and on how financial services can be used by the poor and the vulnerable, especially women, to help them build resilience and adapt to the many challenges— and opportunities—posed by the climate crisis. When it comes to building resilience to climate shocks at the individual and household level, it is essential to consider the role of financial services and how to translate the macro-level climate finance commitments into products and services that can help vulnerable households. It is also important to ensure that efforts to green the financial sector do not come at the expense of inclusive finance products that can help the poor build resilience and improve their livelihoods, including in the face of climate change.

Access to a range of generic financial services already helps build resilience. Reliable savings and remittance products, for example, do not need to be specifically designed for climate risks to help smooth consumption during periods of drought or to help speed recovery after a climate shock. However, other types of products can have a greater impact if they are specifically designed for certain risks. Credit products, for example, can help the poor invest in risk-reduction measures like irrigation, hardier seed varieties, or the transition into new livelihoods and diversified sources of income. Insurance helps poor people handle losses and helps them rebuild lives and livelihoods—and it also helps them become more resilient to the next shock. Adaptive social-protection payments from governments and humanitarian organizations help people survive the immediate aftermath of a climate shock—especially severe and large-scale shocks that vulnerable populations cannot manage on their own.

There are already many examples of financial products that have helped the poor manage climate shocks. During the January 2013 flooding in Mozambique, for example, people in affected areas used their mobile wallets to receive digital money transfers from friends and families. The velocity of these transfers was far greater than that of social-safety-net transfers from the government, or support from informal lenders.

Mobile money enables an informal insurance network that can effectively mitigate against the impact of both individual and macro shocks:

Evolution of Total Value of Monthly Mobile Transfers Received by All Sampled Households in Mozambique

Other examples also illustrate how financial services are helping the poor not only survive climate crises but take the first steps toward longer-term adaptation. Across Africa and parts of Asia, for instance, more than 4 million farmers receive loans and area-yield index insurance through agricultural insurance provider Pula and their many bank partners. The bundled product incentivizes farmers to switch to resilient seeds and protects them in case of climate-related losses. In India, SMV Green Solutions has helped 1,700 rickshaw drivers gain access to loans to purchase e-rickshaws. The e-rickshaws have vastly improved drivers' health compared with manual ferrying; are less expensive, since drivers don't have to buy petrol; and have lower emissions and thus a smaller environmental impact.

Providing Financial Tools for Climate Resilience Is Very Complex

CGAP's Leadership Essay on resilience described the complexity inherent in building resilience to the risks faced by poor people. Climate risk is even more complex than other common risks, and poor people's typical risk-management strategies may not work very well in dealing with climate risks. There are three key aspects that make climate change more complex in a financial inclusion setting.

First, climate shocks are mostly co-variant, meaning that they affect many people simultaneously. This is not the case with most risks that poor people have to manage. This makes traditional sources of resilience, such as informal financial services, unworkable for any significant length of time, since many need to draw on them simultaneously (i.e., not everyone can cash out of the savings group at the same time). Moreover, in times of crisis, formal financial-service providers sometimes suspend their operations. The resilience of any individual depends on the resilience of other people; of informal savings and insurance arrangements; of formal providers of infrastructure, from cellphone towers to agents; and even of government safety nets.

Second, the impact of climate shocks will vary significantly based on the type of shock (especially if it has a slow rather than sudden onset) and the distinct locations of people affected by the shock. For example, city-dwellers affected by a flood will face different challenges and response approaches than rural residents who suffer through a drought that threatens their crops. This means they will also need different financial instruments. That is not the case with other risks such as fire, crime, or illness, where the response mechanisms tend to be similar and where most people use the same set of financial tools to manage the risks.

Third, managing climate shocks is more complex than many other types of risks for vulnerable people, since they are difficult to predict and since they often play out through second- and third-order effects. Figuring out which adaptation response will be most effective, amid a wide range of unpredictable outcomes, is very difficult. For the poor to be truly resilient against the shocks of climate change, they must also have the knowledge, tools, and resources to enable their long-term adaptation. The traditional patterns of livelihoods must adapt amid shifts in temperature, changes in rainfall, increased water scarcity, and continuing ecosystem changes. The need to shift away from traditional livelihoods—or to relocate, fleeing exposed locations — will again disproportionately disrupt the lives of the poor and the vulnerable. Developing financial services that support the poor in this uncertain transition will likewise be complex.

> *"Resolutions like this have a history of laying the foundation for effective treaties and national laws."*

Access to a Healthy Environment Is a Universal Human Right All Countries Must Honor

Joel E. Correia

In this viewpoint Joel E. Correia explains how the United Nations General Assembly's 2022 decision to declare the ability to live in a "clean, healthy, and sustainable environment" a universal human right could lead to future international treaties and laws to support this goal. Even though the UN resolution isn't legally binding and doesn't get too specific in its language, in the past the Universal Declaration of Human Rights played a major role in establishing standards and laws. This resolution will put pressure on all nations to work towards the goal of creating and protecting a healthy environment for all people. Joel E. Correia is an assistant professor of Latin American studies at the University of Florida.

"The UN Declared a Universal Human Right to a Healthy, Sustainable Environment— Here's Where Resolutions Like This Can Lead," by Joel E. Correia, The Conversation, August 5, 2022, https://theconversation.com/the-un-declared-a-universal-human-right-to-a-healthy-sustainable-environment-heres-where-resolutions-like-this-can-lead-188060. Licensed under CC BY-ND 4.0 International.

As you read, consider the following questions:

1. Which rights were included in the first set of universal human rights declared by the UN?
2. What is the "triple planetary crisis"?
3. How did the declaration of the human right to water impact policy?

Climate change is already affecting much of the world's population, with startlingly high temperatures from the Arctic to Australia. Air pollution from wildfires, vehicles and industries threatens human health. Bees and pollinators are dying in unprecedented numbers that may force changes in crop production and food availability.

What do these have in common? They represent the new frontier in human rights.

The United Nations General Assembly voted overwhelmingly on July 28, 2022, to declare the ability to live in "a clean, healthy and sustainable environment" a universal human right. It also called on countries, companies and international organizations to scale up efforts to turn that into reality.

The declaration is not legally binding—countries can vote to support a declaration of rights while not actually supporting those rights in practice. The language is also vague, leaving to interpretation just what a clean, healthy, and sustainable environment is.

Still, it's more than moral posturing. Resolutions like this have a history of laying the foundation for effective treaties and national laws.

I am a geographer who focuses on environmental justice, and much of my research investigates relationships between development-driven environmental change, natural resource use, and human rights. Here are some examples of how similar resolutions have opened doors to stronger actions.

How the Concept of Human Rights Expanded

In 1948, in the aftermath of World War II, the newly formed United Nations adopted the Universal Declaration of Human Rights in response to the atrocities of the Holocaust. The declaration wasn't legally binding, but it established a baseline of rights intended to ensure the conditions for basic human dignity.

That first set of rights included the right to life, religious expression, freedom from slavery, and a standard of living adequate for health and well-being.

Since then, the scope of human rights has been expanded, including several agreements that are legally binding on the countries that ratified them. The UN conventions against torture (1984) and racial discrimination (1965) and on the rights of children (1989) and persons with disabilities (2006) are just a few examples. Today, the International Bill of Human Rights also includes binding agreements on economic, cultural, civil, and political rights.

Today's Triple Planetary Crisis

The world has changed dramatically since the Universal Declaration of Human Rights was written, perhaps most notably with regard to the scale of environmental crises people worldwide face.

Some experts argue that the "triple planetary crisis" of human-driven climate change, widespread biodiversity loss, and unmitigated pollution now threaten to surpass the planetary boundaries necessary to live safely on Earth.

These threats can undermine the right to life, dignity, and health, as can air pollution, contaminated water, and pollution from plastics and chemicals. That is why advocates argued for the UN to declare a right to a clean, healthy, and sustainable environment.

The UN has been discussing the environment as a global concern for over 50 years, and several international treaties over that time have addressed specific environmental concerns, including binding agreements on protecting biodiversity and closing the ozone hole. The 2015 Paris climate agreement to limit global warming is a direct and legally binding outcome of the long struggles that follow initial declarations.

The resolution on the right to a clean, healthy, and sustainable environment was approved without dissent, though eight countries abstained: Belarus, Cambodia, China, Ethiopia, Iran, Kyrgyzstan, Russia, and Syria.

The Human Right to Water

Voluntary human rights declarations can also be instrumental in changing state policy and providing people with new political tools to demand better conditions.

The human right to water is one of the strongest examples of how UN resolutions have been used to shape state policy. The resolution, adopted in 2010, recognizes that access to adequate quantities of clean drinking water and sanitation are necessary to realize all other rights. Diarrheal disease, largely from unsafe drinking water, kills half a million children under age 5 every year.

Human rights advocates used the resolution to help pressure the Mexican government to reform its constitution and adopt a human right to water in 2012. While the concept still faces challenges, the idea of a right to water is also credited with transforming water access in marginalized communities in Bangladesh, Costa Rica, Egypt, and other countries.

The Rights of Indigenous Peoples

The 2007 UN Declaration on the Rights of Indigenous Peoples is another example. It recognizes the specific histories of marginalization, violence, and exploitation that many Indigenous peoples around the world have endured and contemporary human rights violations.

The resolution outlines rights for Indigenous peoples but stops short of recognizing their sovereignty, something many critique as limiting the scope of self-determination. Within these limits, however, several countries have incorporated some of its recommendations. In 2009, Bolivia integrated it into its constitution.

The Declaration on the Rights of Indigenous Peoples discusses a right to free, prior and informed consent about development and industrial projects that would affect Indigenous people. That has been a powerful tool for Indigenous peoples to demand due process through the legal system.

In Canada, Paraguay, and Kenya, Indigenous peoples have used the resolution to help win important legal victories before human rights courts with rulings that have led to land restitution and other legal gains.

Tools for Change

U.N. declarations of human rights are aspirational norms that seek to ensure a more just and equitable world. Even though declarations like this one are not legally binding, they can be vital tools people can use to pressure governments and private companies to protect or improve human well-being.

Change can take time, but I believe this latest declaration of human rights will support climate and environmental justice across the world.

"*Many observers say that policymakers still have the biggest role to play in setting and enforcing emissions targets.*"

Global Climate Agreements Must Require Greater Action from Nations

Lindsay Maizland

In this viewpoint Lindsay Maizland examines the international agreements on climate change that have had the greatest impact, as well as those that have been less successful. The Kyoto Protocol and the Paris Agreement have had important impacts on limiting greenhouse gas emissions from a large number of countries. However, while the Paris Agreement has played an important role im taking stock of emissions on a global scale and setting guidelines for emissions, many experts say the commitments outlined in the Paris Agreement are not enough. There needs to be greater accountability and more ambitious commitments from all countries. Lindsay Maizland is a writer and editor covering international news and climate change.

As you read, consider the following questions:

1. What is required in the 2015 Paris Agreement?
2. Why are countries trying to keep the rise in global temperature below 1.5°C?

"Global Climate Agreements: Successes and Failures," by Lindsay Maizland, Council on Foreign Relations, December 5, 2023. Reproduced with permission.

3. What other forums might be able to more effectively address climate change?

O ver the last several decades, governments have collectively pledged to slow global warming. But despite intensified diplomacy, the world is already facing the consequences of climate change, and they are expected to get worse.

Through the Kyoto Protocol and the Paris Agreement, countries agreed to reduce greenhouse gas emissions, but the amount of carbon dioxide in the atmosphere keeps rising, heating Earth at an alarming rate. Scientists warn that if this warming continues unabated, it could bring environmental catastrophe to much of the world, including staggering sea-level rise, record-breaking droughts and floods, and widespread species loss.

Since negotiating the Paris accord in 2015, many of the 195 countries that are party to the agreement have strengthened their climate commitments, including through pledges on curbing emissions and supporting countries in adapting to the effects of extreme weather, during the annual UN climate conferences known as the Conference of the Parties (COP). However, the absence of U.S. President Joe Biden and Chinese President Xi Jinping from this year's COP28 summit in Dubai, United Arab Emirates (UAE), have raised concerns about future climate commitments from the world's two largest greenhouse gas emitters.

What Are the Most Important International Agreements on Climate Change?

Montreal Protocol, 1987. Though not intended to tackle climate change, the Montreal Protocol was a historic environmental accord that became a model for future diplomacy on the issue. Every country in the world eventually ratified the treaty, which required them to stop producing substances that damage the ozone layer, such as chlorofluorocarbons (CFCs). The protocol has succeeded in eliminating nearly 99 percent of these ozone-depleting substances.

In 2016, parties agreed via the Kigali Amendment to also reduce their production of hydrofluorocarbons (HFCs), powerful greenhouse gases that contribute to climate change.

UN Framework Convention on Climate Change (UNFCCC), 1992. Ratified by 197 countries, including the United States, the landmark accord was the first global treaty to explicitly address climate change. It established an annual forum, known as the Conference of the Parties, or COP, for international discussions aimed at stabilizing the concentration of greenhouse gases in the atmosphere. These meetings produced the Kyoto Protocol and the Paris Agreement.

Kyoto Protocol, 2005. The Kyoto Protocol, adopted in 1997 and entered into force in 2005, was the first legally binding climate treaty. It required developed countries to reduce emissions by an average of 5 percent below 1990 levels, and established a system to monitor countries' progress. But the treaty did not compel developing countries, including major carbon emitters China and India, to take action. The United States signed the agreement in 1998 but never ratified it and later withdrew its signature.

Paris Agreement, 2015. The most significant global climate agreement to date, the Paris Agreement requires all countries to set emissions-reduction pledges. Governments set targets, known as nationally determined contributions (NDCs), with the goals of preventing the global average temperature from rising 2°C (3.6°F) above preindustrial levels and pursuing efforts to keep it below 1.5°C (2.7°F). It also aims to reach global net-zero emissions, where the amount of greenhouse gases emitted equals the amount removed from the atmosphere, in the second half of the century. (This is also known as being climate neutral or carbon neutral.)

The United States, the world's second-largest emitter, was the only country to withdraw from the accord, a move by former President Donald Trump that took effect in November 2020. However, President Joe Biden reentered the United States into the agreement during his first months in office. Three countries have not formally approved the agreement: Iran, Libya, and Yemen.

Is There a Consensus on the Science of Climate Change?

Yes, there is a broad consensus among the scientific community, though some deny that climate change is a problem, including politicians in the United States. When negotiating teams meet for international climate talks, there is "less skepticism about the science and more disagreement about how to set priorities," says David Victor, an international relations professor at the University of California, San Diego. The basic science is that:

- Earth's average temperature is rising at an unprecedented rate;
- human activities, namely the use of fossil fuels—coal, oil, and natural gas—are the primary drivers of this rapid warming and climate change; and,
- continued warming is expected to have harmful effects worldwide.

Data taken from ice cores shows that Earth's average temperature is rising more now than it has in 800,000 years. Scientists say this is largely a result of human activities over the last 150 years, such as burning fossil fuels and deforestation. These activities have dramatically increased the amount of heat-trapping greenhouse gases, primarily carbon dioxide, in the atmosphere, causing the planet to warm.

The Intergovernmental Panel on Climate Change (IPCC), a UN body established in 1988, regularly assesses the latest climate science and produces consensus-based reports for countries.

Why Are Countries Aiming to Keep Global Temperature Rise Below 1.5°C?

Scientists have warned for years of catastrophic environmental consequences if global temperature continues to rise at the current pace. Earth's average temperature has already increased approximately 1.1°C above preindustrial levels, according to a 2021 assessment by the IPCC. The report, drafted by more than 200 scientists from over 60 countries, predicts that the world will reach or exceed 1.5°C of warming within the next two decades even if nations drastically cut emissions immediately.

An earlier, more comprehensive IPCC report summarized the severe effects expected to occur when the global temperature warms by 1.5°C:

- *Heat waves.* Many regions will suffer more hot days, with about 14 percent of people worldwide being exposed to periods of severe heat at least once every five years.
- *Droughts and floods.* Regions will be more susceptible to droughts and floods, making farming more difficult, lowering crop yields, and causing food shortages.
- *Rising seas.* Tens of millions of people live in coastal regions that will be submerged in the coming decades. Small island nations are particularly vulnerable.
- *Ocean changes.* Up to 90 percent of coral reefs will be wiped out, and oceans will become more acidic. The world's fisheries will become far less productive.
- *Arctic ice thaws.* At least once a century, the Arctic will experience a summer with no sea ice, which has not happened in at least 2,000 years. Forty percent of the Arctic's permafrost will thaw by the end of the century.
- *Species loss.* More insects, plants, and vertebrates will be at risk of extinction.

The consequences will be far worse if the 2°C threshold is reached, scientists say. "We're headed toward disaster if we can't get our warming in check and we need to do this very quickly," says Alice C. Hill, CFR senior fellow for energy and the environment.

Which Countries Are Responsible for Climate Change?

The answer depends on who you ask and how you measure emissions. Ever since the first climate talks in the 1990s, officials have debated which countries—developed or developing—are more to blame for climate change and should therefore curb their emissions.

Developing countries argue that developed countries have emitted more greenhouse gases over time. They say these developed countries should now carry more of the burden because they were able to grow their economies without restraint. Indeed, the United States has emitted the most of all time, followed by the European Union (EU).

However, China and India are now among the world's top annual emitters, along with the United States. Developed countries have argued that those countries must do more now to address climate change.

In the context of this debate, major climate agreements have evolved in how they pursue emissions reductions. The Kyoto Protocol required only developed countries to reduce emissions, while the Paris Agreement recognized that climate change is a shared problem and called on all countries to set emissions targets.

What Progress Have Countries Made Since the Paris Agreement?

Every five years, countries are supposed to assess their progress toward implementing the agreement through a process known as the global stocktake. The first of these reports, released in September 2023, warned governments that "the world is not on track to meet the long-term goals of the Paris Agreement."

That said, countries have made some breakthroughs during the annual UN climate summits, such as the landmark commitment to establish the Loss and Damage Fund at COP27 in Sharm el-Sheikh, Egypt. The fund aims to address the inequality of climate change by providing financial assistance to poorer countries, which are often least responsible for global emissions yet most vulnerable to climate disasters. At COP28, countries decided that the fund will be initially housed at the World Bank, with several wealthy countries, such as the United States, Japan, the United Kingdom, and EU members, initially pledging around $430 million combined.

The UAE also pledged $100 million, a move some analysts say may put additional pressure on other high-emitting countries, such as China and Saudi Arabia, to increase their contributions to climate action funding.

Recently, there have been global efforts to cut methane emissions, which account for more than half of human-made warming today because of they higher potency and heat trapping ability within the first few decades of release. The United States and the EU introduced a Global Methane Pledge at COP26, which aims to slash 30 percent of methane emissions levels from 2020 to 2030. At COP28, oil companies announced they would cut their methane emissions from wells and drilling by more than 80 percent by the end of the decade, and the pledge included international monitoring efforts to hold companies accountable. Meanwhile, the United States announced a commitment to reduce methane emissions from the oil and gas industry by nearly 80 percent over the next 15 years.

Are the Commitments Made Under the Paris Agreement Enough?

Most experts say that countries' pledges are not ambitious enough and will not be enacted quickly enough to limit global temperature rise to 1.5°C. The policies of Paris signatories as of late 2022 could result in a 2.7°C (4.9°F) rise by 2100, according to the Climate Action Tracker compiled by Germany-based nonprofits Climate Analytics and the NewClimate Institute.

"The Paris Agreement is not enough. Even at the time of negotiation, it was recognized as not being enough," says CFR's Hill. "It was only a first step, and the expectation was that as time went on, countries would return with greater ambition to cut their emissions."

Since 2015, dozens of countries—including the top emitters—have submitted stronger pledges. For example, President Biden announced in 2021 that the United States will aim to cut emissions by 50 to 52 percent compared to 2005 levels by 2030, doubling former President Barack Obama's commitment. The following year, the U.S. Congress approved legislation that could get the country close to reaching that goal. Meanwhile, the EU pledged to reduce emissions by at least 55 percent compared to 1990 levels by 2030, and China said it aims to reach peak emissions before 2030.

But the world's average temperature will still rise 2.0°C (3.6°F) by 2100 even if countries fully implement their pledges for 2030 and beyond. If the more than one hundred countries that have set or are considering net-zero targets follow through, warming could be limited to 1.8°C (3.2°F), according to the Climate Action Tracker.

What Are the Alternatives to the Paris Agreement?

Some experts foresee the most meaningful climate action happening in other forums. Yale University economist William Nordhaus says that purely voluntary international accords like the Paris Agreement promote free-riding, and are destined to fail. The best way to cut global emissions, he says, would be to have governments negotiate a universal carbon price rather than focus on country emissions limits. Others propose new agreements that apply to specific emissions or sectors to complement the Paris Accord.

"Progress is going to happen not globally with all countries joined together, but in smaller groups and by sector," says Victor, the international relations professor. In recent years, there have been examples of this. The Group of Twenty (G20), representing countries that are responsible for 80 percent of the world's greenhouse gas pollution, has pledged to stop financing new coal-fired power plants abroad and agreed to triple renewable energy capacity by the end of this decade. However, G20 governments have thus far failed to set a deadline to phase out fossil fuels. In 2022, countries in the International Civil Aviation Organization set a goal of achieving net-zero emissions for commercial aviation by 2050. Meanwhile, cities around the world have made their own pledges. In the United States, more than 600 local governments have detailed climate action plans that include emissions-reduction targets.

Industry is also a large source of carbon pollution, and many firms have said they will try to reduce their emissions or become carbon neutral or carbon negative, meaning they would remove more carbon from the atmosphere than they release. And while there remains little to no oversight of corporate emissions, some governments, including that of the United States, are considering requiring large businesses to report their carbon footprint. The Science Based Targets initiative, a UK-based company considered the "gold standard" in validating corporate net-zero plans, says it has certified the plans of over 3,000 firms, and aims to more than triple this total by 2025. Still, analysts say that many challenges remain, including questions over the accounting methods and a lack of transparency in supply chains.

Despite these trends, many observers say that policymakers still have the biggest role to play in setting and enforcing emissions targets. "It's all pretty small relative to governments around the world setting a forceful climate policy," Michael Greenstone, an economics professor at the University of Chicago, tells CFR's Why It Matters podcast.

Periodical and Internet Sources Bibliography

The following articles have been selected to supplement the diverse views presented in this chapter.

Michael Birnbaum, "How a Small Island Got World's Highest Court to Take on Climate Justice," *Washington Post*, March 29, 2023. https://www.washingtonpost.com/climate-solutions/2023/03/29/vanuatu-international-court-un/.

Kasia Cieplak-Mayr von Baldegg, "Stunning Images of Bangladesh on the Brink of Impending Climate Disaster," the *Atlantic*, July 5, 2012. https://www.theatlantic.com/international/archive/2012/07/stunning-images-of-bangladesh-on-the-brink-of-impending-climate-disaster/467523/.

Tilak Doshi, "Climate Change Hurts the Poor: But Not the Way You Think It Does," *Forbes*, October 26, 2023. https://www.forbes.com/sites/tilakdoshi/2023/10/26/climate-change-hurts-the-poor-but-not-the-way-you-think-it-does/?sh=53de4b5a2113.

Rebecca Halleck and Dionne Searcey, "An Oil Company Is Trespassing on Tribal Land in Wisconsin, Justice Dept. Says," *New York Times*, April 10, 2024. https://www.nytimes.com/2024/04/10/climate/line-five-pipeline-amicus-brief.html?searchResultPosition=7.

Ellen Ioanes, "How 2,000 Elderly Swiss Women Won a Landmark Climate Case," *Vox*, April 9, 2024. https://www.vox.com/world-politics/24125621/switzerland-echr-climate-change-human-rights-court.

Katie Myers, "Montana Youth Win a Historic Climate Case," *Wired*, August 19, 2024. https://www.wired.com/story/montana-youth-win-a-historic-climate-case/.

Robin Rose Parker, "How Climate Change and Environmental Justice Are Inextricably Linked," *Washington Post*, June 14, 2022. https://www.washingtonpost.com/magazine/2022/06/14/climate-justice-green-new-deal/.

Aaron Regunberg and David Arkush, "The Case for Prosecuting Fossil Fuel Companies for Homicide," the *New Republic*, March 10, 2024. https://newrepublic.com/article/179624/fossil-fuel-companies-prosecute-climate-homicide.

Lauren Sommer, "Countries Promise Millions for Damages from Climate Change. So How Would That Work?" NPR, December 1, 2023. https://www.npr.org/2023/12/01/1216243518/cop28-loss-damage-fund-climate-change.

Haley Strack, "The 'Feminist Climate Justice' Framework," *New Republic*, January 26, 2024. https://www.nationalreview.com/corner/the-feminist-climate-justice-framework/.

OPPOSING VIEWPOINTS® SERIES

CHAPTER 2

What Responsibility Do Corporations Have for Climate Change?

Chapter Preface

In Chapter 1, the authors examined the role of nations in contributing to climate change. They asked what rich nations that have historically emitted the most greenhouse gases owe poor and developing nations for the damage this has caused. In this chapter, the authors look at the issue of responsibility in another way; they focus on corporations, particularly Big Oil companies.

In the first viewpoint of this chapter, the authors look at how free market ideology affects the way people view responsibility for climate change. Surprisingly they find that when people adhere to a free-market ideology, they tend to oppose policies that would mitigate climate change even when they know the facts about climate change. In this worldview, corporations may have contributed to climate change, but they should not be made to pay for addressing the problem—or even made to stop causing it.

The authors of the next two viewpoints disagree. One viewpoint argues forcefully that not only corporations, but the lifestyles of the super-rich arc responsible and should be held accountable. The other holds Big Oil corporations responsible, not just for actions that contributed to climate change, but for their efforts to confuse the public about the science. This viewpoint looks at legal action that has been taken to hold Big Oil liable.

The fourth viewpoint here continues the argument from a business perspective, but shifts it to the question of what developing nations should be expected to do as they try to grow their economies. It is not fair, this author says, to expect nations that are trying to develop so that their people can have jobs, adequate housing, and acceptable standards of living to put carbon reduction ahead of economic development.

The final viewpoint takes a look at capitalism more broadly and the role of corporations in society within that ideology, arguing that capitalism must evolve in order to meet the challenges of climate change.

> *"We found that free market ideology is a substantial barrier to believing that companies have a responsibility to deal with climate change and supporting government policy toward that purpose."*

Ideology Can Eclipse Science When It Comes to Climate Change Policy

Kerrie L. Unsworth, Sally V. Russell, and Matthew C. Davis

In this excerpted viewpoint the authors describe their research on people's views about corporate responsibility for climate change. They find that free market ideology can be a barrier to enacting policies to address climate change. Furthermore, they found that people who strongly believe in free market ideology and doubt that climate change is impacted by human behavior are especially disinterested in holding corporations accountable. However, the authors assert that convincing people that human behavior does play a role in climate change could help with this to some extent. Kerrie L. Unsworth, Sally V. Russell, and Matthew C. Davis are researchers at the University of Leeds in the United Kingdom.

"Is Dealing with Climate Change a Corporation's Responsibility? A Social Contract Perspective" by Kerrie L. Unsworth, Sally V. Russell, and Matthew C. Davis. National Library of Medicine, August 18, 2016. https://www.ncbi.nlm.nih.gov/pmc/articles/PMC4988990/. Licensed under CC BY.

As you read, consider the following questions:

1. What is corporate responsibility?
2. What is "free market ideology" and how does it influence beliefs about corporate responsibility.
3. What is the social contract, and why do these authors think that it needs to be considered?

In this research, we [...] sought to understand the social contract underlying CSR [corporate social responsibility], particularly with regards to climate change; namely, whether individuals in the community considered companies to be responsible for dealing with climate change and whether they would support government policy on regulating companies to do so. We argued that this was important to more fully understand our conceptualization of CSR. We found that people thought companies and government had a greater duty to deal with climate change compared to individuals/ families, international community, and local associations; that the more an individual believed that humans contributed to climate change the more they held companies responsible to deal with climate change; but that those who believed in a free market were less likely to hold companies responsible or support regulatory policy particularly when they also did not believe in anthropogenic climate change.

We believe these findings are important from both a theoretical and a practical standpoint. Theoretically, most research that has examined antecedents of organizational-level CSR policies has focused on institutional and organizational factors and little empirical research has examined the role that individuals may play (Aguinis and Glavas, 2012; with the exception of individuals as consumers, see e.g., Russell et al., 2016). Of course, this was not explicitly multi-level research, in that we did not measure specific organizational reactions to individuals' perceptions of responsibility, however, we believe that this adds to the growing field of research that is building the micro-foundations of CSR.

Moreover, we found that free market ideology is a substantial barrier to believing that companies have a responsibility to deal with climate change and supporting government policy toward that purpose. Previously, research on free market ideology has focused on the relationship between ideology and belief in anthropogenic climate change (e.g., Heath and Gifford, 2006) and ideology was assumed to be behind country differences in perceptions of CSR (Maignan, 2001). However, we argued that in addition to the mechanistic model (where free market ideology affects belief in climate change which then affects corporate responsibility beliefs), that free market ideology will play an important independent role as a moderator when we also consider the organizational context.

Indeed, we found this to be the case. We found that when free market ideology was weak then even a moderate level of belief in anthropogenic climate change would be associated with a perception that companies should deal with climate change. However, when free market ideology was strong then belief in anthropogenic climate change was very important. The combination of both strong free market ideology and little belief in anthropogenic climate change led to extremely low levels of perceived corporate responsibility to deal with climate change. Although we recognize that the effect size of this moderation is relatively low, given the importance of the topic and the multiplied error variance in moderation variables we believe that this is still an important finding.

A second finding, however, was that free market ideology was more central than we had originally thought. Although we predicted mediated moderation (where free market ideology moderates not only the relationship to the mediator, namely corporate responsibility, but also the relationship to the outcome variable, namely policy support), we found only moderated mediation. In other words, we found only a first stage moderation where free market ideology interacted with climate change beliefs on perceived corporate responsibility to deal with climate change (c.f., Langfred, 2004). We had also expected that free market ideology would interact with climate change beliefs to influence policy support, but instead we found only the indirect effect (via responsibility) and a direct main effect. Although this component of our hypothesis was not supported, we believe that it signals the strength of the effect of free market ideology. Even a strong belief in anthropogenic climate change is not able to moderate the effect of free market ideology on policy support. In other words, convincing people about anthropogenic climate change may result in increased perceptions of corporate responsibility even for those with a strong free market ideology and this may have some knock-on effect to policy support, but it will have only a limited impact on this outcome in buffering the overall effects of free market ideology.

Policy-makers therefore face an uphill battle in regulating organizations to be more environmentally responsible. Although the government was seen as just as responsible as corporations for dealing with climate change (presumably because of their ability to create policy), their task will not be easy. It is not enough to convince the community that climate change is real and that human activity is causing it. While this will help to some extent, its effect, particularly on policy, may well be limited. Those with a strong free market ideology will likely be those embedded within the capitalist system and potentially constitute a number of stakeholders both politically and organizationally. While some research has shown that demonstrating scientific consensus can counteract the negative effects of free market ideology on beliefs in climate change (Lewandowsky et al., 2013), it is unlikely that it will affect their views on policy support given the lack of interaction we found in our research. Instead, if regulatory environmental policy aimed at companies is desired, then other forms of engagement will be required.

It is important to acknowledge the limitations of our research and in doing so provide fruitful avenues for future research. The first limitation of our research is the cross-sectional nature of the design. This design was appropriate for our purpose of investigating the relationships in our study but we are unable to demonstrate causality between variables. It is not known, for example if a strong free-market ideology acts as an attention bias for scientific evidence on climate change. Such a bias may explain why there is a negative relationship between free-market ideology and belief in anthropogenic climate change. More knowledge of the direction of causality may enable future researchers and practitioners to design more effective campaigns to raise understanding and knowledge of anthropogenic climate change, and motivate future action.

The second limitation of research concerns the sample used in our study. Whilst this was a broad sample of Australian individuals and reflected the political diversity of the country, we must acknowledge the potential for culture to influence individuals' perceptions regarding the implications of, and required action in response to, climate change (e.g., Lorenzoni and Pidgeon, 2006). Future research exploring the consistency of our findings in other countries, particularly those with more collectivist cultures or where environmental regulation of organizations is more stringent, would further our understanding of contextual contingencies and enable the design of more tailored campaigns. Finally, the measures used in our study displayed some limitations. The measure of anthropogenic climate change did not distinguish between those who did not believe in climate change at all and those who believed in naturally caused climate change; the measure of support for climate change regulation did not distinguish between those who supported any regulation and those who supported climate change regulation in particular; and the reliability of the free market ideology measure, while adequate, was not as high as one would ideally like.

Nonetheless, our research may be useful for policy makers and practitioners in their efforts to encourage future climate change action. Indeed, it may be that interventions designed to change behavior may need to ensure that they are concordant with the target's ideology. Research suggests that goal concordance may be an important consideration in the success of pro-environmental behavior change interventions (Unsworth et al., 2013). In this way, for those individuals with a free market ideology it may be more important to appeal to economic goals and present a strong business case, rather than attempting to change their belief in anthropogenic climate change.

Our study reinforces the need to consider the social contract and, in particular, individual citizens and employees when examining the antecedents to organizational-level CSR (Carroll, 2004). The positive relationship between belief in anthropogenic climate change and beliefs that corporates are responsible for dealing with climate change and regulation to that end underlines the role that ordinary citizens may play in shaping the political and regulatory environment in which organizations operate. Our findings further illustrate the complexity of the challenge facing policy makers seeking to introduce environmental regulation, with free market ideology appearing to be a barrier to holding organizations responsible or supporting regulatory policy. This suggests that designing interventions and campaigns that pursue action on climate change will require multidisciplinary input (c.f., Kilbourne et al., 2002; Davis et al., 2014), e.g., from economists and political scientists as well as psychologists, in order to capitalize on non-environmental goals and present credible economic arguments that can appeal to those whose belief in the "invisible hand" is strong.

> *"Beyond the carbon footprint of their rich and famous lifestyles, so called 'carbon billionaires' are making significant financial investments into wealthy corporate polluters."*

Big Oil, Rich Countries, and Carbon Billionaires Are Responsible for Climate Change—and Getting Away with It

Oxfam America

The previous viewpoint found that commitment to a free-market economy can cause people to ignore the realities of climate change. Here, the author explains exactly who is responsible for the problem: Big Oil, rich industrialized countries, and billionaires who engage in activities with high carbon footprints and invest in corporate polluters. The author argues that those responsible for climate change owe communities struggling with the impacts of climate change for the damage they've caused. Oxfam is an international organization dedicated to the alleviation of global poverty and to holding to account those responsible for climate change.

As you read, consider the following questions:

1. According to this viewpoint, who is most responsible for climate change?

"Who is responsible for climate change?" by Oxfam America, December 3, 2023. Reproduced with permission.

2. When did global inequality begin to dramatically increase?
3. What role do the super-rich play in global warming? What are "carbon billionaires"?

The effects of climate change are all too visible in daily life. From heat waves in California to floods in Pakistan, extreme weather and rising temperatures are forcing people from their homes and worsening world hunger and famine.

But the climate crisis neither affects everyone equally—nor is everyone equally responsible. New Oxfam research finds that the richest among us were responsible for more carbon emissions than 5 billion people—the equivalent of 66 percent of humanity—in 2019.

"People who have contributed least to the climate crisis are right now suffering its worst impacts," said Elizabeth Wathuti, a Kenyan climate activist.

At Oxfam, we've been holding wealthy polluters accountable for years. So we're going to explain who is responsible for climate change—Big Oil, rich industrialized countries, and carbon billionaires—and what they owe the people and frontline communities that are paying the heaviest price for their actions.

Big Oil Knowingly Made Climate Change Worse

Wealthy corporations are responsible for recklessly extracting fossil fuels for energy production after centuries of dirty industrialization in Europe and North America—significantly contributing to global climate change.

- According to a three-part PBS FRONTLINE series, Big Oil giant ExxonMobil sat on research by its own scientists conducted in the 1980s showing the connection between fossil fuel activities and global temperature rise.
- With government support, Big Oil doubled down on its polluting exploits, enabling the release of large amounts of carbon dioxide and methane into the earth's atmosphere.

- Approximately 71 percent of carbon emissions can be traced to just 100 fossil fuel producers since 1988.

By the mid '90s, a global scientific consensus emerged that humans were contributing to global temperature rise. But Big Oil—led by its lobbyists at groups like the American Petroleum Institute—did everything it could to seed doubt and delay meaningful climate action in the U.S. and globally.

Rich Industrialized Countries Have Contributed the Most Historical Emissions to Climate Change

Before the early 1800s, individuals worldwide had more similar living standards. The Industrial Revolution in the Global North changed everything, and global economic inequality grew substantially among people around the world through the middle of the 20th century.

So what was the climate impact of that transformation?

- A *New York Times* analysis found that 23 rich industrialized countries are responsible for 50 percent of all historical emissions and more than 150 countries are responsible for the rest.
- According to former NASA scientist James Hansen, industrialization in Europe, North America, Australia, and Japan was responsible for 77 percent of global emissions between 1751–2006.

Though China is responsible for the largest percentage of current emissions, rich industrialized countries are still responsible for more than one third. By comparison, Africa's current emissions are less than 4 percent of the global total.

"Wealthy countries are disproportionately responsible for the climate crisis, and they have the double responsibility to both cut emissions at home and to support developing countries with the costs of replanting crops and rebuilding homes after storms, and moving from dirty energy forms to cleaner, lower-carbon ones," said Oxfam's Climate Policy Lead Nafkote Dabi.

The Right to a Clean Environment Is a Basic Right

The Constitution of India being the supreme law of the nation lays down several rights, duties and principles that each individual must abide by. Majority of constitutional provisions provide a collection of core or inherent rights that apply to all people. These are designed with the purpose of constraining the authority that the Sovereign has upon its citizens and its obligation of defending their integrity as persons. Part III of the Indian Constitution defines the fundamental rights that the citizens of the nation can exercise while certain rights are available to all the people regardless of their nationality, these include the basic right to life, personal liberty and equality before law.

Article 21 of the Indian Constitution grants right to life, personal liberty that is available to each and every individual. Decent standard of living and a pollution free environment is an inherent part of the right to life.

Our legal system acknowledges that the right to a clean environment is indeed a very old concept recognized by the judiciary. That is a basic right as well. There have been various legal rulings in support of this right. The government's and every Indian citizen's primary responsibility is to safeguard the environment. Articles 21, 14, and 19 have been applied to environmental stewardship. The privilege of living with dignity includes the ability to live in a safe environment. However, considering the present case scenario, our environment is not just sustainable for living but is on the verge of deteriorating day by day, that would in turn pose a threat over our right to life since one cannot sustain without the existence of a clean and safe environment. This raises a concern to ensure a clean and safe environment and the measures to ensure the same have also been initiated by various judicial pronouncements.

"Constitutional Recognition of Environmental Protection in India" by Mahi Pandit. Elsevier, August 14, 2023.

Carbon Billionaires Are Propping Up Fossil Fuels with Their Investments

The super-rich—the top 1 percent of global population by income—bear their own responsibility for climate change. Beyond the carbon footprint of their rich and famous lifestyles, so called "carbon billionaires" are making significant financial investments into wealthy corporate polluters, according to Oxfam research.

- These 125 billionaires are responsible for emitting an average of 3 million carbon tons each year.
- From 1990–2015, the carbon emissions of the super-rich globally were more than double the emissions of the poorest half of humanity. Over that same time, the poorest 50 percent—around 3.1 billion people—were responsible for just 7 percent of emissions.
- Emissions of the super-rich will cause 1.3 million heat-related deaths between 2020 and 2030—roughly the equivalent of the entire population of Dallas.

"The major and growing responsibility of wealthy people for overall emissions is rarely discussed or considered in climate policy making," Dabi said. "This has to change. These billionaire investors at the top of the corporate pyramid have huge responsibility for driving climate breakdown. They have escaped accountability for too long."

Conclusion

These wealthy polluters are responsible for climate change—and it's time to hold them accountable on the world stage.

Big Oil must stop exploiting communities that possess natural resources in the Global South as the transition to clean energy continues, rich industrialized countries must pay for the loss and damage already being experienced by communities on the frontlines of the crisis, and carbon billionaires must shift their investments to funds with stronger environmental and social standards.

VIEWPOINT 3

> "Local and state governments that are suing want to hold the major oil companies responsible for the costs of responding to disasters that scientists are increasingly able to attribute to climate disruption and tie back to the fossil fuel industry."

Big Oil Must Be Held Accountable

Patrick Parenteau and John Dernbach

In this viewpoint Patrick Parenteau and John Dernbach discuss how U.S. cities, counties, and states have started suing the oil industry over the impacts of climate change. At the time this viewpoint was published in 2023, over a dozen local and state governments had sued oil companies like Sunoco LP and Exxon Mobil Corp. A ruling by the U.S. Supreme Court helped give these cases by state and local governments a chance by asserting that the cases should be heard at the state level rather than the federal level, which gives governments a better likelihood of winning these cases. While these potential victories may be more symbolic rather than financially beneficial, it would set an important precedent in holding oil companies legally responsible for the impacts of climate change. Patrick Parenteau is a professor emeritus of law at Vermont Law and Graduate School.

John Dernbech is a professor emeritus of law at Widener University in Pennsylvania.

As you read, consider the following questions:

1. How much property value is at risk of being lost to rising sea levels by 2100 in Honolulu?
2. Why do the authors say Big Oil companies "lost one of their most powerful arguments" due to a Supreme Court ruling?
3. Why do the authors believe these legal cases matter even though the verdicts are unlikely to come anywhere near covering the cost of damages?

H onolulu has lost more than five miles of its famous beaches to sea level rise and storm surges. Sunny-day flooding during high tides makes many city roads impassable, and water mains for the public drinking water system are corroding from salt water because of sea level rise.

The damage has left the city and county spending millions of dollars on repairs and infrastructure to try to adapt to the rising risks.

Future costs will almost certainly be higher. More than US$19 billion in property value, at today's dollars, is at risk by 2100 from projected sea level rise, driven by greenhouse gas emissions largely from the burning of fossil fuels. Elsewhere in Honolulu County, which covers all of Oahu, many coastal communities will be cut off or uninhabitable.

Unwilling to have their taxpayers bear the full brunt of these costs, the city and county sued Sunoco LP, Exxon Mobil Corp., and other big oil companies in 2020.

Their case—one of more than two dozen involving U.S. cities, counties and states suing the oil industry over climate change—just got a break from the U.S. Supreme Court. That has significantly increased their odds of succeeding.

Suing Over the Cost of Climate Change

At stake in all of these cases is who pays for the staggering cost of a changing climate.

Local and state governments that are suing want to hold the major oil companies responsible for the costs of responding to disasters that scientists are increasingly able to attribute to climate disruption and tie back to the fossil fuel industry. Several of the plaintiffs accuse the companies of lying to the public about their products' risks in violation of state or local consumer protection laws that prohibit false advertising.

The governments in the Honolulu case allege that the oil companies "are directly responsible" for a substantial rise in carbon dioxide emissions that have been driving climate change. They say the companies should contribute their fair share to defray some of the costs.

The gist of Honolulu's complaint is that the big oil companies have known for decades that their products cause climate change, yet their public statements continued to sow doubts about what was known, and they failed to warn their customers, investors and the public about the dangers posed by their products.

Were it not for this deception, the lawsuit says, the city and county would not be facing mounting costs of abating the damage from climate change.

Importantly, the complaint is based on state—not federal—law. It alleges that the defendants have violated established common law rules long recognized by the courts involving nuisance, failure to warn, and trespass.

The city and county want the companies to help fund climate adaptation measures—verything from building seawalls and raising buildings to buying flood-prone properties and restoring beaches and dunes.

Supreme Court Could Have Killed These Cases

Not surprisingly, the oil companies have thrown their vast legal resources into fighting these cases.

On April 24, however, they lost one of their most powerful arguments.

The U.S. Supreme Court declined to hear challenges in the Hawaii case and four others involving the seemingly technical question of which court should hear these cases: state or federal.

The oil companies had "removed" the cases from state court to federal court, arguing that damage lawsuits for climate change go beyond the limits of state law and are governed by federal law.

That theory would have derailed all five cases – because there is no federal common law for greenhouse gases.

The court made that position clear in 2011 in *American Electric Power Co. v. Connecticut*. Several state and local governments had sued five major power companies for violating the federal common law of interstate nuisance and asked for a court order forcing these companies to reduce their emissions. The Supreme Court refused, holding that the federal Clean Air Act displaced federal common law for these gases.

In *Native Village of Kivalina v. Exxon Mobil Corp.*, a federal court of appeals extended that holding to also bar claims for monetary damages based on federal common law.

To avoid this fate, Honolulu and the other plaintiffs focused on violations of state law, not federal law. Without exception, the federal courts of appeals sided with them and sent the cases back to state court.

What Happens Next?

The Honolulu case leads the pack at this point.

In 2022, the 1st Circuit Court in Hawaii denied the oil companies' motion to dismiss the case based on the argument that the Clean Air Act also preempts state common law. This could open the door for discovery to begin sometime this year.

In discovery, senior corporate officers – perhaps including former Exxon Mobil CEO Rex Tillerson, who was secretary of state under Donald Trump – will be required to answer questions under oath about what the companies knew about climate change versus what they disclosed to the public.

Evidence from Exxon documents, described in a recent study by science historians Naomi Oreskes and Geoffrey Supran, shows that the company's own scientists "knew as much as academic and government scientists knew" about climate change going back decades. But instead of communicating what they knew, "Exxon worked to deny it," Supran and Oreskes write. The company overemphasized uncertainties and cast doubt on climate models.

This is the kind of evidence that could sway a jury. The standard of proof in a civil case like Honolulu's is "preponderance of the evidence," which roughly translates to 51%. Ten of the 12 jurors must agree on a verdict.

Any verdict likely would be appealed, perhaps all the way to the U.S. Supreme Court, and it could be years before the Honolulu case is resolved.

Lawsuits Don't Begin to Cover the Damage

It is unlikely that even substantial verdicts in these cases will come close to covering the full costs of damage from climate change.

According to the National Oceanic and Atmospheric Administration, in 2022 alone the U.S. sustained 18 weather and climate disasters that each exceeded $1 billion in damage. Together, they cost over $165 billion.

But for many of the communities most at risk from these disasters, every penny counts. We believe establishing the oil companies' responsibility may also discourage further investments in fossil fuel production by banks and brokerage houses already nervous about the financial risks of climate disruption.

> *"We believe the blunt exclusion of all nonrenewable energy projects from development finance is an inequitable and ineffective climate strategy that gaslights over 1 billion Africans."*

Banning Financing for Fossil Fuel Projects in Africa Won't Solve Climate Change or Inequality

Benjamin Attia and Morgan Bazilian

In this viewpoint Benjamin Attia and Morgan Bazilian discuss the trend of wealthy countries vowing to cease public funding for fossil fuel projects in less developed countries while continuing to finance and subsidize these projects in their own countries. The authors argue it is easier for countries to make these rules for overseas financing rather than domestic financing, but that this ultimately will not have a huge impact on carbon emissions but will have a considerable negative impact on the development of poorer countries. The authors assert that many developing countries, such as those in sub-Saharan Africa, will likely make use of many renewable energy sources, but there are some regions where electric grids are necessary for development, and the income generated from fossil fuel extraction is important to their development as well. Benjamin Attia is a fellow

"Why Banning Financing for Fossil Fuel Projects in Africa Isn't a Climate Solution," by Benjamin Attia and Morgan Bazilian, The Conversation, October 14, 2021, https://theconversation.com/why-banning-financing-for-fossil-fuel-projects-in-africa-isnt-a-climate-solution-169220. Licensed under CC BY-ND 4.0 International.

at the Payne Institute for Public Policy at Colorado School of Mines, where Morgan Bazilian is a professor of public policy and director of the Payne Institute.

As you read, consider the following questions:

1. What percent of sub-Saharan Africans have no access to electricity?
2. How does the number of gas-fired power plants and coal plants in the U.S., U.K., European Union, Japan, and Russia compare to the number in sub-Saharan Africa?
3. Why did Nigerian Vice President Yemi Osinbajo consider "climate transition" a term that shouldn't be applied universally?

Today's global energy inequities are staggering. Video gamers in California consume more electricity than entire nations. The average Tanzanian used only one-sixth the electricity consumed by a typical American refrigerator in 2014.

Globally, the top 10% of countries consume 20 times more energy than the bottom 10%. And 1.1 billion sub-Saharan Africans share the same amount of power generation capacity as Germany's 83 million people. At least half have no access to electricity at all.

These stark energy inequalities are fueling thorny debates around financing Africa's energy future as world leaders and their negotiators meet at COP26, the United Nations climate conference in Glasgow, Scotland.

One increasingly common theme primarily from wealthy countries – including those responsible for the majority of greenhouse gas emissions over time – is a vow that they will cease public funding for all (or nearly all) fossil fuel projects in less developed countries, even as they continue financing, and in many cases heavily subsidizing, fossil fuels in their own.

It is generally easier for countries that offer overseas development finance for energy projects to make low-carbon rules for others, rather than for themselves. For example, China and Japan – two high coal-consuming nations – have recently pledged to stop funding coal projects overseas and increase investments in renewables. But they have made no equivalent commitments at home. The list of countries committing to phase out coal in the next two decades grew to over 40 during the UN climate conference in November, but China, Japan, the U.S. and several other major coal users weren't on it.

Another group of 25 countries and development finance institutions pledged to stop most public investment in unabated fossil fuel projects, including oil and natural gas, outside their borders by the end of 2022, but many of the countries still support fossil fuels at home.

The U.S. Treasury and the United Kingdom's development finance institution, CDC Group – both countries are involved in the new pledge – have recently taken a more nuanced approach by limiting support for overseas coal and oil-based power generation projects but leaving a narrow window available for natural gas projects in poor countries that pass a rigorous screening process. This is roughly similar to the approach of the World Bank.

As experienced clean energy policy researchers, we believe the blunt exclusion of all nonrenewable energy projects from development finance is an inequitable and ineffective climate strategy that gaslights over 1 billion Africans.

Tiny Climate Gains, Major Development Losses

Focusing on limiting the emissions of the world's poorest countries while emissions continue to rise in industrialized countries is clearly misdirected in our view. Given stark inequalities in energy use and emissions, this could instead entrench poverty and widen inequality induced by worsening climate change, while simultaneously accomplishing very little to reduce global greenhouse gas emissions.

Together, the U.S., U.K., European Union, Japan and Russia have almost the same population – 1.1 billion people – as sub-Saharan Africa, but 35 times more gas-fired power plants in operation or under development, and 52 times more coal plants.

When it comes to carbon dioxide emissions, sub-Saharan Africa is collectively responsible for barely half a percent of all global emissions over time, while the U.S., U.K., E.U., Japan and Russia are responsible for more than 100 times that amount, or about 57%.

The upper bound for Africa's future growth in power sector emissions is also negligible. If the region's electricity demand hypothetically tripled tomorrow, rather than doubling by 2040 as the International Energy Agency recently forecast, and if only natural gas was used to meet the new demand, annual global emissions would increase by only 0.62%, according to one estimate. That's equivalent to the state of Louisiana's annual emissions today.

What's more, the share of renewable power in many sub-Saharan African national grids is already higher than for nearly all the big greenhouse gas emitters. In at least six countries – Kenya, Ethiopia, Malawi, Mali, Mozambique and Uganda – renewables make up more than 50% of their annual generation. In 2018, hydropower, geothermal, solar and wind made up about 20% of the continent's total power generated.

Most of the region will find renewable power to be the fastest and cheapest way to expand their generation capacity, but some areas may still need to rely on some fossil fuels in various sectors of the economy as they develop.

It has been clear for decades that the world needs to rapidly and aggressively cut its greenhouse gas emissions to keep global warming below 1.5 degrees Celsius and avoid the worst impacts of climate change. Many regions in Africa, including the Sahel and Mozambique, are already facing the effects of climate change, including worsening droughts, food insecurity and severe storms. Adapting to climate change and building resilience requires the very energy, economic development and infrastructure currently lacking in some of the most affected regions and those least prepared to adapt.

Climate Colonialism and Legacies of Colonization

Other experts agree that this direction of climate policy is not just ineffective, it's rooted in the historic inequities of colonialism.

The philosopher Olúfẹ́mi O. Táíwò defines climate colonialism as the "deepening or expansion of foreign domination through climate initiatives that exploits poorer nations' resources or otherwise compromises their sovereignty."

Colonialism's legacy is a contributing factor to a wide range of issues, from conflict to corruption, and to the poor state of electricity access across much of Africa today.

While industrializing nations in the 1900s were building electricity grids through massive public spending campaigns, like Franklin Roosevelt's New Deal in the United States and the Electricity Supply Act of 1926 in the U.K., most of Africa was being actively pilfered of its rich natural resources. Much of the infrastructure built in colonial Africa during that time was built only to facilitate resource extraction operations, such as mined commodities, oil, timber, rubber, tea, coffee and spices.

In 1992, a coalition of low-income nations successfully advocated for the U.N.'s climate mitigation pathways to include their right to development, and a "common but differentiated responsibility" to address the dual problems of development and climate change. This language has long been the basis of equity considerations in climate policy, including in the 2015 Paris Agreement, which expects deeper emissions cuts from developed countries based on their "respective capabilities."

A Transition from What?

Nigerian Vice President Yemi Osinbajo recently described "energy transition" as "a curious term" when applied universally, given the energy shortfalls in countries like Nigeria. He has argued for an energy transition in which Africa can develop quickly and grow.

Increasing electricity in industrializing regions of sub-Saharan Africa would first power income-generating activities and public services, both drivers of economic growth.

Equitable and effective climate negotiations will require nuanced policy considerations that balance the priorities of alleviating energy poverty with urgent climate change mitigation and adaptation. A just energy transition would leave African governments to make and implement policies and deliver on their own national climate commitments under the Paris Agreement rather than shouldering the West's.

> *"The problem with the pernicious notion that a corporation's sole purpose is to serve shareholders is that it leads to many other undesirable outcomes."*

Capitalism Can and Must Evolve to Meet the Challenges of Climate Change

Andrew J. Hoffman

In this viewpoint Andrew J. Hoffman examines the different roles capitalism plays in climate change. Many people hold it responsible for the rampant consumerism that has led to climate change, while others argue that the free market will guide us to solutions for problems like climate change. Capitalism is not an unchanging entity that is free from government influence—it often has had to change to address societal issues, and this often happens through government regulation. Hoffman argues that corporations can't solely exist to make money for shareholders, that instead they must consider the ethical outcomes of their actions. Through thoughtful leadership and a shift in priorities that focuses on the welfare of future generations, corporations and capitalism as a whole can help address the challenges of climate change. Andrew J. Hoffman is the Holcim (U.S.) Professor of Sustainable Enterprise at the University of Michigan, where he teaches in the School of Environment and Sustainability and the Ross School of Business.

As you read, consider the following questions:

1. According to this viewpoint, why are more conservative-leaning people skeptical of climate change?
2. What are some ways in which capitalism has already evolved to meet the needs of society?
3. What are ways in which it is harmful for corporations to focus solely on profit?

There are two extremes in the debate over capitalism's role in our present climate change problem. On the one hand, some people see climate change as the outcome of a consumerist market system run rampant. In the end, the result will be a call to replace capitalism with a new system that will correct our present ills with regulations to curb market excesses.

On the other hand, some people have faith in a free market to yield the needed solutions to our social problems. In the more extreme case, some see climate policy as a covert way for bigger government to interfere in the market and diminish citizens' personal freedom.

Between these two extremes, the public debate takes on its usual binary, black-and-white, conflict-oriented, unproductive and basically incorrect form. Such a debate feeds into a growing distrust many have for capitalism.

A 2013 survey found that only 54% of Americans had a positive view of the term, and in many ways both the Occupy and Tea Party movements share similar distrust in the macro-institutions of our society to serve everyone fairly; one focuses its ire at government, the other at big business, and both distrust what they see as a cozy relationship between the two.

This polar framing also feeds into culture wars that are taking place in our country. Studies have shown that conservative-leaning people are more likely to be skeptical of climate change, due in part to a belief that this would necessitate controls on industry and commerce, a future they do not want. Indeed, research has shown a strong correlation between support for free-market ideology and rejection of climate science. Conversely, liberal-leaning people are more likely to believe in climate change because, in part, solutions are consistent with resentment toward commerce and industry and the damage they cause to society.

This binary framing masks the real questions we face, both what we need to do and how we are going to get there. Yet there are serious conversations within management education, research and practice about the next steps in the evolution of capitalism. The goal is to develop a more sophisticated notion of the role of the corporation within society. These discussions are being driven not only by climate change, but concerns raised by the financial crisis, growing income inequality and other serious social issues.

The Market's Rough Edges

Capitalism is a set of institutions for structuring our commerce and interaction. It is not, as some think, some sort of natural state that exists free from government intrusion. It is designed by human beings in the service of human beings and it can evolve to the needs of human beings. As Yuval Levin points out in National Affairs, even Adam Smith argued that "the rules of the market are not self-legislating or naturally obvious. On the contrary, Smith argued, the market is a public institution that requires rules imposed upon it by legislators who understand its workings and its benefits."

And, it is worth noting, capitalism has been quite successful. Over the past century, the world's population increased by a factor of four, the world economy increased by a factor of 14 and global per capita income tripled. In that time, average life expectancy increased by almost two-thirds due in large part to advances in medicine, shelter, food production and other amenities provided by the market economy.

Capitalism is, in fact, quite malleable to meet the needs of society as they emerge. Over time, regulation has evolved to address emergent issues such as monopoly power, collusion, price-fixing and a host of other impediments to the needs of society. Today, one of those needs is responding to climate change.

The question is not whether capitalism works or doesn't work. The question is how it can and will evolve to address the new challenges we face as a society. Or, as Anand Giridharadas pointed out at the Aspen Action Forum, "Capitalism's rough edges must be sanded and its surplus fruit shared, but the underlying system must never be questioned."

These rough edges need be considered with the theories we use to understand and teach the market. In addition, we need to reconsider the metrics we use to measure its outcomes, and the ways in which the market has deviated from its intended form.

Homo economicus?

To begin, there are growing questions around the underlying theories and models used to understand, explain, and set policies for the market. Two that have received significant attention are neoclassical economics and principal-agent theory. Both theories form the foundation of management education and practice and are built on extreme and rather dismal simplifications of human beings as largely untrustworthy and driven by avarice, greed, and selfishness.

As regards neoclassical economics, Eric Beinhocker and Nick Hanauer explain:

> Behavioral economists have accumulated a mountain of evidence showing that real humans don't behave as a rational homo economicus would. Experimental economists have raised awkward questions about the very existence of utility; and that is problematic because it has long been the device economists use to show that markets maximize social welfare. Empirical economists have identified anomalies suggesting that financial markets aren't always efficient.

As regards principal-agent theory, Lynn Stout goes so far to say that the model is quite simply "wrong." The Cornell professor of business and law argues that its central premise—that those running the company (agents) will shirk or even steal from the owner (principal) since they do the work and the owner gets the profits—does not capture "the reality of modern public corporations with thousands of shareholders, scores of executives, and a dozen or more directors."

The most pernicious outcome of these models is the idea that the purpose of the corporation is to "make money for its shareholders." This is a rather recent idea that began to take hold within business only in the 1970s and 1980s and has now become a taken-for-granted assumption.

If I asked any business school student (and perhaps any American) to complete the sentence, "the purpose of the corporation is to…" they would parrot "make money for the shareholder." But that is not what a company does, and most executives would tell you so. Companies transform ideas and innovation into products and services that serve the needs of some segment of the market. In the words of Paul Pollman, CEO of Unilever, "business is here to serve society." Profit is the metric for how well they do that.

The problem with the pernicious notion that a corporation's sole purpose is to serve shareholders is that it leads to many other undesirable outcomes. For example, it leads to an increased focus on quarterly earnings and short-term share price swings; it limits the latitude of strategic thinking by decreasing focus on long-term investment and strategic planning; and it rewards only the type of shareholder who, in the words of Lynn Stout, is "shortsighted, opportunistic, willing to impose external costs, and indifferent to ethics and others' welfare."

A Better Way to Gauge the Economy

Going beyond our understanding of what motivates people and organizations within the market, there is growing attention to the metrics that guide the outcomes of that action. One of those metrics is the discount rate. Economist Nicholas Stern stirred a healthy controversy when he used an unusually low discount rate when calculating the future costs and benefits of climate change mitigation and adaptation, arguing that there is a ethical component to this metric's use. For example, a common discount rate of 5 percent leads to a conclusion that everything 20 years out and beyond is worthless. When gauging the response to climate change, is that an outcome that anyone—particularly anyone with children or grandchildren—would consider ethical?

Another metric is gross domestic product (GDP), the foremost economic indicator of national economic progress. It is a measure of all financial transactions for products and services. But one problem is that it does not acknowledge (nor value) a distinction between those transactions that add to the well-being of a country and those that diminish it. Any activity in which money changes hands will register as GDP growth. GDP treats the recovery from natural disasters as economic gain; GDP increases with polluting activities and then again with pollution cleanup; and it treats all depletion of natural capital as income, even when the depreciation of that capital asset can limit future growth.

A second problem with GDP is that it is not a metric dealing with true human well-being at all. Instead, it is based on the tacit assumption that the more money and wealth we have, the better off we are. But that's been challenged by numerous studies.

As a result, French ex-president Nicolas Sarkozy created a commission, headed by Joseph Stieglitz and Amartya Sen (both Nobel laureates), to examine alternatives to GDP. Their report recommended a shift in economic emphasis from simply the production of goods to a broader measure of overall well-being that would include measures for categories like health, education, and security. It also called for greater focus on the societal effects of income inequality, new ways to measure the economic impact of sustainability and ways to include the value of wealth to be passed on to the next generation. Similarly, the king of Bhutan has developed a GDP alternative called gross national happiness, which is a composite of indicators that are much more directly related to human well-being than monetary measures.

The form of capitalism we have today has evolved over centuries to reflect growing needs, but also has been warped by private interests. Yuval Levin points out that some key moral features of Adam Smith's political economy have been corrupted in more recent times, most notably by "a growing collusion between government and large corporations." This issue has become most vivid after the financial crisis and the failed policies that both preceded and succeeded that watershed event. The answers, as Auden Schendler and Mark Trexler point out, are both "policy solutions" and "corporations to advocate for those solutions."

We Can Never Have a Clean Slate

How will we get to the solutions for climate change? Let's face it. Installing efficient LED light bulbs, driving the latest Tesla electric car, and recycling our waste are admirable and desirable activities. But they are not going to solve the climate problem by reducing our collective emissions to a necessary level. To achieve that goal requires systemic change. To that end, some argue for creating a new system to replace capitalism. For example, Naomi Klein calls for "shredding the free-market ideology that has dominated the global economy for more than three decades."

Klein is performing a valuable service with her call for extreme action. She, like Bill McKibben and his 350.org movement, is helping to make it possible for a conversation to take place over the magnitude of the challenge before us through what is called the "radical flank effect."

All members and ideas of a social movement are viewed in contrast to others, and extreme positions can make other ideas and organizations seem more reasonable to movement opponents. For example, when Martin Luther King Jr. first began speaking his message, it was perceived as too radical for the majority of white America. But when Malcolm X entered the debate, he pulled the radical flank further out and made King's message look more moderate by comparison. Capturing this sentiment, Russell Train, second administrator of the EPA, once quipped, "Thank God for [environmentalist] Dave Brower; he makes it so easy for the rest of us to be reasonable."

But the nature of social change never allows us the clean slate that makes sweeping statements for radical change attractive. Every set of institutions by which society is structured evolved from some set of structures that preceded it. Stephen Jay Gould made this point quite powerfully in his essay "The Creation Myths of Cooperstown," where he pointed out that baseball was not invented by Abner Doubleday in Cooperstown, New York, in 1839. In fact, he points out, "no one invented baseball at any moment or in any spot." It evolved from games that came before it. In a similar way, Adam Smith did not invent capitalism in 1776 with his book *The Wealth of Nations*. He was writing about changes that he was observing and had been taking place for centuries in European economies; most notably the division of labor and the improvements in efficiency and quality of production that were the result.

In the same way, we cannot simply invent a new system to replace capitalism. Whatever form of commerce and interchange we adopt must evolve out of the form we have at the present. There is simply no other way.

But one particularly difficult challenge of climate change is that, unlike Adam Smith's proverbial butcher, brewer or baker who provide our dinner out of the clear alignment of their self-interest and our needs, climate change breaks the link between action and outcome in profound ways. A person or corporation cannot learn about climate change through direct experience. We cannot feel an increase in global mean temperature; we cannot see, smell, or taste greenhouse gases; and we cannot link an individual weather anomaly with global climate shifts.

A real appreciation of the issue requires an understanding of large-scale systems through "big data" models. Moreover, both the knowledge of these models and an appreciation for how they work require deep scientific knowledge about complex dynamic systems and the ways in which feedback loops in the climate system, time delays, accumulations, and nonlinearities operate within them. Therefore, the evolution of capitalism to address climate change must, in many ways, be based on trust, belief and faith in stakeholders outside the normal exchange of commerce. To get to the next iteration of this centuries-old institution, we must envision the market through all components that help to establish the rules; corporations, government, civil society, scientists and others.

The Evolving Role of the Corporation in Society

At the end of the day, the solutions to climate change must come from the market and more specifically, from business. The market is the most powerful institution on earth, and business is the most powerful entity within it. Business makes the goods and services we rely upon: the clothes we wear, the food we eat, the forms of mobility we use, and the buildings we live and work in.

Businesses can transcend national boundaries and possess resources that exceed that of many countries. You can lament that fact, but it is a fact. If business does not lead the way toward solutions for a carbon-neutral world, there will be no solutions.

Capitalism can, indeed it must, evolve to address our current climate crisis. This cannot happen through either wiping clean the institutions that presently exist or relying on the benevolence of a *laissez faire* market. It will require thoughtful leaders creating a thoughtfully structured market.

Periodical and Internet Sources Bibliography

The following articles have been selected to supplement the diverse views presented in this chapter.

Emma Farge, "UN Declares Access to a Clean Environment a Human Right," Reuters, October 8, 2021. https://www.reuters.com/business/environment/un-passes-resolution-making-clean-environment-access-human-right-2021-10-08/.

Christiana Figueres, "Solving Climate Change Requires A New Social Contract," *Time*, January 20, 2022. https://time.com/6140430/climate-change-trust/.

Shannon Hall, "Exxon Knew About Climate Change Almost 40 Years Ago," *Scientific American,* October 26, 2015. https://www.scientificamerican.com/article/exxon-knew-about-climate-change-almost-40-years-ago/.

Christopher M. Matthews, "Inside Exxon's Strategy to Downplay Climate Change," *Wall Street Journal*, September 14, 2023. https://www.wsj.com/business/energy-oil/exxon-climate-change-documents-e2e9e6af.

Dharna Noor and Oliver Milman, "Fury after Exxon Chief Says Public to Blame for Climate Failures," the *Guardian*, March 4, 2024. https://www.theguardian.com/us-news/2024/mar/04/exxon-chief-public-climate-failures.

Wayne Parry, "New Jersey Voters May Soon Decide Whether They Have a Right to a Clean Environment," PBS/WHYY, March 15, 2024. https://whyy.org/articles/new-jersey-environmental-vote-pollution/.

Adele Peters, "Oil Companies Owe the World Trillions in Climate Reparations. This Study Calculates the Exact Cost," *Fast Company*, May 19, 2023. https://www.fastcompany.com/90898704/oil-companies-owe-the-world-trillions-in-climate-reparations.

Heather Souvaine Horn, "Exxon Wants You to Feel Guilty About Climate Change," *New Republic*, March 7, 2024. https://newrepublic.com/post/179609/exxon-ceo-darren-woods-blames-consumers-climate-change.

Daniel Willis, "What Big Oil Owes the World," Global Justice Now, February 25, 2023. https://www.globaljustice.org.uk/blog/2023/02/what-big-oil-owes-the-world/.

Katarina Zimmer, "A Healthy Environment as a Human Right," *Knowable Magazine*, April 20, 2021. https://knowablemagazine.org/content/article/society/2021/a-healthy-environment-human-right.

OPPOSING
VIEWPOINTS®
SERIES

CHAPTER 3

What Role Should Social Justice Play in Decisions About Climate Change?

Chapter Preface

Poor nations are disproportionally harmed by climate change, as we have seen in earlier chapters. However, poor and otherwise marginalized groups within poor and rich countries alike suffer more from the ravages of climate change. In this chapter, the authors look at the problem as a whole, and then zero in on specific populations being harmed.

The first viewpoint explains how the climate crisis's impact on water-related disasters such as droughts and floods has put vulnerable populations around the world in even more precarious positions and advocates for more people from these countries having a voice in conversations about potential solutions.

The next viewpoint looks at how climate change is setting back decades of progress in lifting people out of poverty and suggests ways to limit the damage.

In the third viewpoint, the authors recommend five strategies to minimize the loss and damage climate change visits upon vulnerable communities. These strategies include working closely with those communities and getting their input on possible responses. In the next viewpoint, the author explains why climate justice and social justice are inextricably intertwined, or as she puts it, "two sides of the same coin." She focuses her analysis particularly on Middle East North Africa (MENA), a region of the world that is warming at twice the global average.

The last two viewpoints look specifically at women, girls, and gender-diverse people, arguing that gender inequality and climate change are interconnected, too.

> *"Water insecurity—including everything from a lack of drinking water to the threat of homes being swept away—can have serious implications for people's wellbeing."*

The Impacts of Climate Change Affect Marginalized Communities More

Tahseen Jafry

In this viewpoint Tahseen Jafry explains how climate change has caused a number of water-related crises—such as drought, hurricanes, and floods—in countries around the world. She also points out that the number of people without access to clean drinking water has increased over the past three decades. Often it is poorer countries and marginalized populations that are most impacted by water insecurity. Development aid and donations have historically played a significant role in helping countries and populations address this issue, but Jafry asserts that strong government leadership is necessary to promote coordination and long-term investment in securing these resources. Tahseen Jafry is the Director of the Mary Robinson Centre for Climate Justice at Glasgow Caledonian University in Scotland.

"Billions Still Lack Access to Safe Drinking Water—This Is a Global Human Rights Catastrophe," by Tahseen Jafry, The Conversation, April 17, 2023, https://theconversation.com/billions-still-lack-access-to-safe-drinking-water-this-is-a-global-human-rights-catastrophe-202564. Licensed under CC BY-ND 4.0 International.

As you read, consider the following questions:

1. What percent of the world's population doesn't have access to clean drinking water?
2. Is access to clean drinking water considered a human right in all places, according to this viewpoint?
3. What positive news does Jafry share about the pursuit of clean water for all?

Leaders and authorities recently gathered in New York for the first UN water conference in decades. The hope was that there would be some landmark breakthroughs to ensure that everyone had access to safe drinking water and sanitation.

The UN secretary-general, António Guterres, called for member states to "bring the water action agenda to life" through developing resilient infrastructure, water pipelines, and waste water treatment plans and putting in place early warning systems against natural disasters.

But if such pledges are not supported by guaranteed funds as well as legally binding legislation—and they aren't—they risk undermining the energy and enthusiasm required to achieve the UN's own sustainable development goal of making access to clean water a human right.

Climate change and related droughts, hurricanes, floods, and other extreme weather events are making it harder to access water for human consumption. In some parts of the world such as the Horn of Africa, the wells have run dry and there simply isn't enough rain any more. The region is experiencing its worst drought for 40 years.

In places where floods are a bigger risk than droughts, such as the U.S. state of Mississippi or parts of Kenya, supplies of fresh water have been contaminated by floodwater filled with agricultural pollutants and industrial chemicals.

Water insecurity—including everything from a lack of drinking water to the threat of homes being swept away—can have serious implications for people's wellbeing. Flood victims in Pakistan have experienced post-traumatic stress disorder, for instance. All this means clean water has become a source of widespread climate injustice, especially in the most vulnerable countries.

Alarmingly there are more people now without access to clean water than there were three decades ago. In 2022 the State of the World's Drinking Water report by the WHO, UNICEF, and the World Bank, noted that one-quarter of the world's population is left without access to safe drinking water. People in sub-Saharan Africa haven't benefited from investment and have the lowest levels of access.

In many poorer countries, access to drinking water is not recognised as a basic human right. Research I published with colleagues on water access in two of those countries, Malawi and Zambia, found that water was neither privatised nor a state provision.

People in these countries instead relied on development aid and donor funding to sink bore holes or provide water pumps in rural areas, and if there was no aid they had to organise clean water themselves on a small community basis. Many pumps and wells do not work, or they are vandalised, and as a result many find themselves drinking unclean water.

In such countries there is lots of wrangling between politicians, traditional leaders, and communities over who actually owns or should govern water points. Many different actors are involved, including public and private organisations, NGOs, faith-based organsations, and donors. This all makes the job of providing water even less straightforward, and coordinating these different actors is paramount.

This lack of coordination, combined with an over-reliance on donors and a lack of local input in decision-making leads me to wonder at what point will access to water actually become a national priority in water insecure countries.

Governments need to take a leading role by facilitating long-term investment in the sector and promoting initiatives which incorporate the right to water access. Solutions to water access should be part of a broader socioeconomic development model which promotes awareness around rights and responsibilities.

Ultimately the management of water resources lies with the governments, who retain a sovereign duty to ensure the human right to safe drinking water. The water crisis is a climate justice crisis. What is needed is commitment in terms of real funding, not just pledges, to ensure that these basic human rights are exercised with support from the United Nations.

Some good news did emerge from the conference in New York, including calls for the UN to appoint a special envoy for water, and a Water Action Agenda containing 700 commitments. Member states, development banks, large companies, and NGOs have all pledged to direct millions of pounds to the water sector.

But just as a village in Malawi might suffer from a lack of coordination between different actors who want to develop a local well, the same problem risks happening on a global scale. What's really needed is strong leadership so all sectors work collectively to ensure everyone in the world really does have access to clean water.

> *"By hitting the poorest hardest, climate change risks both increasing existing economic inequalities and causing people to fall into poverty."*

Climate Change Is Setting Back Progress in Reducing Global Inequality

Céline Guivarch, Nicolas Taconet, and Aurélie Méjean

This viewpoint begins with the good news: Global economic growth has lifted millions out of poverty. The bad news is that climate change is rapidly setting that progress back. Climate change puts many people's health and livelihoods at risk and amplifies existing inequality. These authors detail who is affected, why, and what can be done to mitigate the damage and explain how climate change and inequality are inextricably linked. Céline Guivarch, Nicolas Taconet, and Aurélie Méjean are researchers at the International Center for Research on Environment and Development in Nogent-sur-Marne, France.

As you read, consider the following questions:

1. How might actions to slow global warming have the unintended effect of increasing inequality?

"Linking Climate and Inequality," Céline Guivarch, Nicolas Taconet, and Aurélie Méjean, International Monetary Fund, September 2021. Reproduced with permission.

2. Why are the poor especially vulnerable to climate change, according to this viewpoint?
3. Why do poor populations need a voice in determining global warming mitigation and adaptation strategies?

In recent decades, global economic growth has lifted millions out of extreme poverty and reduced inequalities between countries. But unmanaged climate change threatens to set back that progress by damaging poverty eradication efforts worldwide, and disproportionately affecting the poorest regions and people.

The evidence is mounting: a World Bank report estimated that an additional 68 to 135 million people could be pushed into poverty by 2030 because of climate change. Our own research shows that if the most dire projections of future economic damages in the current scientific literature hold true, climate change would reverse the gains of the past few decades and cause inequality between countries to rise again. Within countries, the impacts of climate change also risk worsening inequality.

At the same time, actions taken to curb warming could have an unwelcome effect on inequality, if climate policies prove too burdensome for poor countries. Such actions need to be complemented by measures to offset the costs on the poor and vulnerable across and within countries.

We view mitigating climate change as a necessary condition for sustainably improving living standards around the world. At the same time, we maintain that distributive and procedural justice must be at the forefront of every stage of environmental policymaking. In planning, development, and implementation, the effort to reduce emissions must be at the service of broader objectives of development, such as poverty and inequality reduction, the creation of decent jobs, improvement of air quality, and improvement of public health.

Risk to Health and Livelihoods

Since the Industrial Revolution, emissions of greenhouse gases due to human activities have increased from a negligible level to more than 40 billion tons a year. As these emissions have accumulated in our atmosphere, they have increased the average annual temperature by about 1 degree Celsius compared with the pre-industrial era. Temperature increases have led to glaciers and ice caps melting, sea levels rising, and more frequent and extreme meteorological events, such as heat waves and droughts, with cascading effects on ecosystems, agricultural yields, human health, and livelihoods.

While the effects of climate change are global, and their projected impacts concern every area in the world, a wide scientific literature suggests that climate risks disproportionately affect the poorest countries and people, who are more exposed and more vulnerable to their impacts.

In the poorest economies, a large part of the population depends directly on activities that may be the most affected by climate change, notably, the agricultural, forestry, and fisheries sectors. People with the lowest incomes are the most likely to depend for their survival on resources provided by nature. Rising temperatures are exacerbating preexisting disparities in access to clean water and affordable food. Most of the time, the poorest populations do not benefit from insurance mechanisms or have access to basic health services, making them particularly vulnerable to any shock hitting their assets and income streams.

Rich Countries and People

And it is the populations of these economies most vulnerable to climate change who contribute the least to the accumulation of greenhouse gases.

Greenhouse gas emissions today are mainly linked to the level of a nation's wealth: the richest countries represent only 16 percent of the world population but almost 40 percent of CO_2 emissions. The two categories of the poorest countries in the World Bank classification account for nearly 60 percent of the world's population, but for less than 15 percent of emissions. On a per capita basis, emissions are about 20 metric tons of CO2-equivalent a person a year in the United States—approximately double the amount per person in the European Union or in China, and almost 10 times the amount in India.

This cross-country inequality is rooted in history: the contribution of the developed economies to global warming is greater than their share of current emissions because they have added to the accumulation of greenhouse gases in the atmosphere for a longer period. For example, the contribution of the United States to cumulative emissions is 25 percent of the total, the European Union's 22 percent, China's 13 percent, and India's 3 percent.

Reducing Inequalities

Without action to limit and adapt to climate change, its environmental impact will continue to amplify inequalities and could undermine development and poverty eradication. While inequality refers to differences in income or wealth across the whole range distribution, poverty concerns individuals below a given income threshold, or lacking access to basic needs. By hitting the poorest hardest, climate change risks both increasing existing economic inequalities and causing people to fall into poverty.

Limiting the global temperature increase to 1.5°C requires reaching net zero CO_2 emissions by 2050 and reducing global emissions by approximately 50 percent in 2030, compared with 2010 levels. Limiting the increase in temperature to 2°C means net zero CO_2 emissions should be reached by 2070, and global emissions should be reduced by 25 percent by 2030. Every fraction of a degree counts because the impacts of climate change increase with rising temperature in a nonlinear way. For instance, while an increase of 1.5°C would expose 245 million people to a new or aggravated water shortage, this number becomes 490 million at +2°C.

The Link Between Climate Change, Poverty, and Inequality

At Oxfam, we know that climate change, poverty, and inequality are linked. The impact of shifting weather patterns, droughts, flooding, and storms hits marginalized communities with few resources first and worst, causing unpredictable growing seasons, crop failures, and sharp increases in food prices. People in low-and lower-middle-income countries are around five times more likely than people in high-income countries to be displaced by sudden extreme weather disasters; and long standing gender, racial, and economic inequalities mean that historically marginalized communities are the hardest hit and most impacted by the climate crisis.

Climate change contributes to fragility and the risk of conflict and disaster. Climate-fueled disasters were the number one driver of internal displacement over the last decade—forcing an estimated 32 million people from their homes in 2022 alone. Hunger is already increasing due to climate change. People are being forced from their livelihoods, homes, and communities due to climate shocks and persistent climate stress—indigenous peoples being among those at greatest risk of displacement. Climate change increases the need for life-saving assistance and protection for those facing humanitarian disasters.

We also know that climate change has worsened global inequality. Across societies, the impacts of climate change affect women and men differently. Women and girls must walk farther to collect water and fuel and are often the last to eat. During and after extreme weather events, they are at increased risk of violence and exploitation. These inequalities can be seen in many other, often overlapping, dimensions too. And because Black, Brown, and Indigenous communities are more likely to live in poverty, they face these impacts while having fewer resources to respond to climate-induced natural disasters and adapt to changes in the climate.

Our collective response to combat climate change must not only address the climate impacts, but also deliver systemic transformation that centers environmental justice in order to address the climate crisis as well as economic, gender, and racial injustice. We are dedicated to working with these communities to prepare for disasters and build resilience to adapt and find long-term solutions to climate change.

"Climate change and inequality" by Oxfam America Inc.

The need is urgent for policies to transform rapidly and profoundly the way we use energy and transportation, produce and consume food as well as other goods, and shelter ourselves. The question is how to design these policies.

Mitigation Efforts

Reducing emissions will ultimately limit climate change impacts and their unequal effects; however, mitigation policies must not neglect their own impacts on inequalities. As they affect energy or food prices, mitigation policies may also slow down progress in energy access and affect the poorest, who spend a higher share of income on these goods.

Thus, mitigation efforts should be shared fairly to ensure they serve the broader objectives of development, poverty, and inequality reduction, improvement of air quality, health, and so forth. Given their greater historical contribution and greater ability to pay for mitigation, rich countries should pave the way by taking ambitious climate action. Financial transfers between countries can also reduce the burden of mitigation for poorer countries and increase participation in mitigation efforts.

Within regions and countries, policy design is key to making sure climate policies do not hurt the poorest. For instance, redistribution plans for the revenues generated by carbon prices can offset the negative impacts on poor people and even lead to net benefits for the poorest. Conversely, concerns about the regressive effects of policies have prevented strengthening existing carbon tax levels, for instance in France following the Yellow Vest movement. Other policies, such as investment in low-carbon technologies or building standards, can also have unequal effects on individuals, depending on their design.

Promoting Adaptation and Resilience

In parallel to reducing emissions, adaptation policies must be put in place to decrease the exposure of the most vulnerable populations to climate change impacts. This means devising rules regulating construction in risky areas, such as flood zoning, land entitlement, and building standards. The poorest communities must be provided with better health services and new insurance mechanisms.

As the poorest tend to be excluded from the decision-making process, there is always a risk of underinvestment in actions that would be particularly beneficial to them. Policies need to be tailored to ensure they do not impose undue financial constraints on those who have the fewest resources. Policymakers must guarantee that adaptation policies will actually benefit those most in need and will not be hijacked by the wealthiest or by political interests.

Another idea of interest is the creation of adaptation funds that would ensure technological transfers from rich countries, which produce most patents, to poorer ones.

Increasing countries' mitigation ambitions will be the main topic of the United Nations Climate Change Conference of the Parties (COP26) on November 1–12. The success of those negotiations is a precondition to limiting inequality-exacerbating climate change. At the same time, careful attention to the equity and fairness of actions for vastly unequal countries will be key for the success of the negotiations themselves.

Jointly tackling climate change and inequality reductions requires paying attention to the intricate links between these issues. Limiting climate change is essential to reduce the risks it would impose, notably on the poorest. However, to design climate policies, the recognition that individuals and countries differ in their ability to mitigate emissions and to cope with climate change impacts is essential. Poorly designed policies risk amplifying existing inequalities, but just transitions to low carbon and more resilient economies can foster more equal societies.

> *"To understand climate risk it is therefore critical to understand people's sense of loss and to co-produce strategies to minimize these."*

Losses and Damage Can Be Lessened by Working with Vulnerable Communities

Jon Barnett and Arghya Sinha Roy

As other viewpoints have stated, vulnerable communities suffer loss and damage from climate change at a higher rate than wealthier countries. In this viewpoint, the authors suggest five ways to minimize that damage. Keeping vulnerable populations involved in adaptation efforts and putting people first are essential for successful adaptation, according to the authors. Jon Barnett is a professor in the School of Geography, Earth and Atmospheric Sciences at Melbourne University in Australia. Arghya Sinha Roy is principal climate change specialist in the Climate Change and Sustainable Development Department of the Asian Development Blog.

As you read, consider the following questions:

1. What are the differences between "hard" and "soft" limits to adaptation, as described here?

Jon Barnett, Arghya Sinha Roy, "Five Innovative Strategies to Minimize Loss and Damage from Climate Change," Asian Development Blog (ADB), November 7, 2023. Reprinted with permission.

2. Why do these authors think it is crucial to empower vulnerable communities?

3. What are "co-drivers" and why do they need to be taken into account when crafting climate policies?

The adverse impacts of climate change are being felt across Asia and the Pacific. For example, the 2022 floods in Pakistan cost the economy $30 billion, and in 2018 Cyclone Gita caused damages equivalent to 38 percent of Tonga's gross domestic product.

However, climate impacts are not only caused by extreme events, they are also caused by slow-onset climate trends. For example, in Fiji coastal erosion is causing villages to relocate to higher ground.

The science is clear that without deep cuts in emissions and improved adaptation processes these impacts will amplify, and it is the most vulnerable—such as rural farmers, fishers, and informal workers in cities—that will be most impacted.

Rapidly increasing climate risk means we are fast approaching the "limits" to adaptation, leading to increasing loss and damage. This includes both economic and non-economic losses, the latter including the loss of lives, lands, sacred places, community cohesion, and cultural traditions.

While some of the limits to adaptation are "hard" and can only be avoided by more ambitious climate mitigation, many of the limits are "soft" and can be pushed with more ambitious climate adaptation. Minimizing losses requires urgent action to push the limits to adaptation.

These five strategies will help push the soft limits to adaptation to minimize loss and damage.

First, adopt people-centered approach in understanding climate risk. Non-economic losses often reflect the intersection of people's relationships with their environment and society. To understand climate risk it is therefore critical to understand people's sense of loss and to co-produce strategies to minimize these.

This approach can empower vulnerable communities, foster collective action, and build a sense of care and responsibility in adaptation efforts. Strong partnerships between government, technical organizations and community-based organizations will be critical for success. This new generation of people-centered assessment can be promoted as part of multi-hazard risk assessments.

Second, adaptation pathways should guide decision-making. Adaptation entails adjusting long-standing development processes and institutions that may be no longer fit for purpose in a changing climate. Developed in a participatory manner, adaptation pathways help us understand when adaptation needs to happen. This involves starting small and preparing for change to be implemented at key moments as climate changes.

The process involves identifying climate tipping points, developing plans to minimize the impact of these, and socialising alternative responses in advance. Developing adaptation pathways also provides an opportunity to work with developing countries so that they own the processes for building long-term resilience, including through strategic plans that transcend individual investments, improved governance, and political and financial commitment. Adaptation pathways also provide opportunities for long-term programmatic financing that is needed to build resilience.

Third, increase investments in ecosystem and nature-based solutions. Compared to climate change, human uses of the environment are often more responsible for stresses in vulnerable ecosystems. For example, in riparian and wetland ecosystems, human diversions of water are often a larger driver of change than climate. In coastal areas, poorly sited and designed structures can have a bigger impact on erosion than sea-level rise.

In these cases, the limits to adaptation are 'soft' in the sense that loss and damage can be averted with improved practices in natural resources management so that ecosystems are more resilient to climate stressors. In addition, investments in infrastructure that work with biological and ecological processes to reduce vulnerability to climate risks such as coastal erosion and urban heating can also deliver efficient and more sustainable adaptation outcomes.

Thus, investments in such ecosystem and nature-based adaptation can help minimize loss and damage to people who depend on climate-sensitive ecosystems for their welfare.

Fourth, investments in human and social development will be critical to reduce vulnerability to climate risk. Climate risk is shaped by environmental and sociocultural processes. For example, the effects of climate change on hunger is due to many co-drivers that increase vulnerability, including marginalization of women from decision-making in households, and secondary malnutrition due to lack of access to quality water supply.

While adaptation is frequently a matter of local actions, co-drivers often emanate from deeply rooted sociocultural institutions that reduce people's choices to adapt, including those associated with gender norms, conflict, caste, and land use. Recognition of the multiple drivers of vulnerability, however, also means there are multiple options to push the limits of adaptation.

Examples include incorporating adaptive features in social protection systems so they help build households' capacity to adapt and better respond to climate events. Decentralization of programs to improve the participation of poor and marginalized people in resilience-related decision-making processes is also important. Such strategies enhance the choices people have to adapt to climate change in ways that minimize what they would consider to be intolerable losses and damages.

Fifth, establish systems to continuously learn from and innovate from the experiences gained in implementing adaptation solutions on the ground. A key limit to adaptation in any given place is simply a lack of knowledge about what can be done effectively to reduce climate risk, which is continuously changing.

To better adapt to climate change, we need to learn from successful examples and see adaptation as a continuous journey towards climate resilience. Being innovative and knowledgeable about adaptation is key to improving our ability to adapt. Regularly reviewing and assessing previous adaptation efforts can help us learn what works best and understand how to do it effectively.

So too does establishing institutional systems that adopt participatory processes for monitoring changes in people's immediate environments and daily lives.

Implementing these five strategies can minimize the impacts of loss and damage through investments in climate adaptation and resilience.

> *"The climate crisis is making existing inequalities and injustices a whole lot worse."*

Climate Justice and Social Justice Are Two Sides of the Same Coin

Ghiwa Nakat

This viewpoint by Ghiwa Nakat makes explicit the connection between climate justice and social justice and focuses on parts of the world and populations that are being hit especially hard by climate change. She explains how the Middle East North Africa region has had compounding crises, including the COVID pandemic, conflict, economic issues, social problems, and natural disasters. The water scarcity caused by climate change has only exacerbated these issues. Climate justice must involve helping these countries adapt to the effects of climate change, giving vulnerable populations a voice in discussions about climate change adaptation, and ultimately moving away from fossil fuel extraction. Ghiwa Nakat is the executive director of Greenpeace Middle East North Africa (MENA).

As you read, consider the following questions:

1. What area of the world mentioned in this viewpoint is warming at twice the global average?

"Climate justice and social justice: Two sides of the same coin" by Ghiwa Nakat. Greenpeace, February 21, 2023. Reproduced with permission.

2. What examples does Nakat give of marginalized communities being hit hard by the effects of climate change?

3. What solution does this author offer?

Climate justice and social justice are two sides of the same coin. Addressing both is vital to creating a more equitable and sustainable future for all. Climate justice is rooted in recognising that climate change is causing a multitude of detrimental social, economic, health, and other impacts on vulnerable communities who have contributed the least to the climate crisis. In short, the climate crisis is making existing inequalities and injustices a whole lot worse.

Low-income countries, people of colour, Indigenous People, women, and people with disabilities are more exposed to the devastating impacts of climate disasters such as floods, wildfires, severe drought, and soaring temperatures, as well as rising sea levels and limited access to food and water. This global majority—marginalised and made more vulnerable by powerful systems of oppression—don't have access to the financial resources and institutional capacity to adapt to climate change nor to recover from the losses and damage that it causes.

The cost of loss and damage is estimated to be between 290 to 580 billion USD per year by 2030 and unfortunately, much of this will be shouldered by developing and least developed countries.

Why Climate Justice Matters

Why does climate justice matter? It matters because it forces the global community and those who bear most responsibility for the climate crisis to work with and support those bearing its brunt. It matters because it addresses a more systemic problem that is the fundamental cause of this crisis and many others. The problem is an economic model based on extractivism and greed that's causing a planetary crisis and aggravating social injustices around the world.

While the whole world, and more specifically the Middle East North Africa region where I live, struggles with compounding crises—triggered by conflicts, pandemic, social and economic problems, deteriorating living conditions and devastating disasters—big western oil firms, by far some of the largest contributors to the global climate crisis, more than doubled their profits to 219 billion USD in 2022.

MENA is the most water scarce region in the world, and is already warming at twice the global average. Vulnerable communities are now suffering the impact of climate change disproportionately to other parts of the world, whether they are living in deserts or beside the sea, on mountains or in green valleys.

This region is facing scorching temperatures that pose a direct risk to human health, as well as longer and more severe droughts with serious implications for agriculture and food security. More frequent climate-related disasters are considerably increasing social inequalities and crippling social justice. Lives are being lost, homes destroyed, crops are failing, livelihoods are jeopardised, and cultural heritage is being wiped out.

Bearing Witness

At Greenpeace MENA we have witnessed and documented how climate change is putting the region's entire ecosystem, civilization, people, and heritage at risk. In Morocco, the increasing drying and loss of the oasis ecosystem are threatening the traditional nomadic lifestyle of indigenous people who depend on it. Studies show that olive trees and olive oil production from Egypt to Lebanon is being significantly impacted by rising temperatures. Threats of flooding along the Mediterranean coast are becoming ever more pressing. Ahwari women in Southern Iraq marshlands are the first to suffer from climate change that caused crops to fail, and limited access to water which made it difficult for them to raise and earn a livelihood and support their families, perpetuating the cycle of poverty and inequality.

Again and again, we are seeing that the communities most vulnerable to these impacts are also those with the lowest resilience in socioeconomic terms. Climate justice is vital to addressing social justice.

Make Polluters Pay

Achieving both climate and social justice, requires addressing the historic and ongoing injustices that have contributed to the current existential climate crisis, and empowering local communities to participate in the climate decision-making processes. It requires acknowledging that historical polluting countries and industries are responsible for the crisis the world is facing—and that those who contributed the least to the problem are now suffering most.

It starts by holding polluting corporations and countries accountable and demanding them to pay for the damage they have caused and continue to cause.

Fossil fuels are responsible for over 75 percent of global GHG emissions and 90 percent of CO2 emissions. There is no climate justice without a just phase out of all fossil fuels: coal, oil, and gas. The only path to a sustainable and resilient world—and to achieve the social and climate justice we all need—is by adopting an alternative economic model that moves quickly away from its addiction to fossil energy, and places people and sustainability over profits and extractivism.

By prioritising climate justice, we can achieve social justice and create a more equitable and sustainable future for all. This is why climate justice matters.

Take action now to end fossil fuel crimes and make polluters pay.

> "The climate crisis is not 'gender neutral.' Women and girls experience the greatest impacts of climate change, which amplifies existing gender inequalities and poses unique threats to their livelihoods, health, and safety."

Gender Inequality and Climate Change Are Interconnected

UN Women

This viewpoint, published on International Women's Day 2022 by UN Women, looks at the deep connection between gender inequality and climate change. Societal gender inequities such as less access to resources and information for women and increased responsibility for caring for the family put women at greater risk of losing their lives in climate disasters. Women who are also part of other marginalized populations—such as Indigenous women, women of color, and LGBTQIA+ women—are hit even harder. UN Women is a part of the United Nations (UN) that is dedicated to gender equality and the empowerment of women.

As you read, consider the following questions:

1. What employment sector is the most important for women in low and lower-middle income countries?
2. What is meant by a "threat multiplier"?
3. How does climate change make it harder for girls to attend school?

Gender inequality coupled with the climate crisis is one of the greatest challenges of our time. It poses threats to ways of life, livelihoods, health, safety, and security for women and girls around the world.

Historically, climate change scientists, researchers, and policymakers have struggled with how to make the vital connections between gender, social equity, and climate change. As more and more data and research reveal their clear correlation, it's time to talk about the disparate impacts of climate change and the linkages between women's empowerment and effective, global climate action.

On International Women's Day, we take a look at how climate change impacts women and girls, why gender equality is key to climate action, and what you can do to support solutions for women, by women.

How Does Climate Change Impact Women and Girls?

The climate crisis is not "gender neutral". Women and girls experience the greatest impacts of climate change, which amplifies existing gender inequalities and poses unique threats to their livelihoods, health, and safety.

Across the world, women depend more on, yet have less access to, natural resources. In many regions, women bear a disproportionate responsibility for securing food, water, and fuel. Agriculture is the most important employment sector for women in low- and lower-middle income countries, during periods of drought and erratic rainfall, women, as agricultural workers and primary procurers, work harder to secure income and resources for their families. This puts added pressure on girls, who often have to leave school to help their mothers manage the increased burden.

Climate change is a "threat multiplier", meaning it escalates social, political, and economic tensions in fragile and conflict-affected settings. As climate change drives conflict across the world, women and girls face increased vulnerabilities to all forms of gender-based violence, including conflict-related sexual violence, human trafficking, child marriage, and other forms of violence.

When disasters strike, women are less likely to survive and more likely to be injured due to long standing gender inequalities that have created disparities in information, mobility, decision-making, and access to resources and training. In the aftermath, women and girls are less able to access relief and assistance, further threatening their livelihoods, wellbeing and recovery, and creating a vicious cycle of vulnerability to future disasters.

Women's and girls' health is endangered by climate change and disasters by limiting access to services and health care, as well as increasing risks related to maternal and child health. Research indicates that extreme heat increases incidence of stillbirth, and climate change is increasing the spread of vector-borne illnesses such as malaria, dengue fever, and Zika virus, which are linked to worse maternal and neonatal outcomes.

How Does Climate Change Intersect with Other Inequalities for Women and Girls?

While women and girls experience disproportionate impacts from climate change at the global level, the effects are not uniform. Looking at climate change through the lens of intersectional feminism, the way in which various forms of inequality often operate together and exacerbate each other, it is clear that climate change risks are acute for Indigenous and Afro-descendent women and girls, older women, LGBTIQ+ people, women and girls with disabilities, migrant women, and those living in rural, remote, conflict and disaster-prone areas.

"If you are invisible in everyday life, your needs will not be thought of, let alone addressed, in a crisis situation," says Matcha Phorn-In, a lesbian feminist human-rights defender who works to empower stateless and landless Indigenous women, girls and young LGBTIQ+ people in Thailand's Chiang Mai, Mae Hong Son, and Tak provinces. "Humanitarian programmes tend to be heteronormative and can reinforce the patriarchal structure of society if they do not take into account sexual and gender diversity," Phorn-In explains. "In addressing structural change, we are advocating for and working towards equality of all kinds."

In the Brazilian Amazon, Dandara Rudsan, a Black and trans activist and an environmental racism specialist in the Public Defender's Office of Pará State, knows firsthand that centering the experiences and challenges faced by different groups illuminates the connections between all fights for justice and liberation.

"In the Amazon, defending human rights means fighting for the survival of people and the rain forest every day, but there is no hierarchy between agendas... To finance social movements in the Amazon is to finance the survival of these communities, these people, and the rainforest."

> "Women are acutely impacted by environmental crises because they experience pre-existing social and economic disadvantage. Another reason is they tend to take responsibility for caring for other vulnerable groups, such as children or older people."

Women and Gender-Diverse People Are Much More Likely to Die in Climate Disasters than Men

Carla Pascoe Leahy

In this viewpoint Carla Pascoe Leahy explains how research indicates that women and gender-diverse people are significantly more likely to be harmed or die from extreme weather events caused by climate change. Much of the research focuses on these impacts on women and gender-diverse people in Australia, where the author is from, but touches on this pattern in other countries as well. Leahy argues that in order to help protect women and other people who are socially marginalized survive the impacts of climate change, more women and gender-diverse people need to have leadership positions. They are not helpless victims, but rather have very important insights into how the issue of climate change adaptation can be approached. Carla Pascoe Leahy is an adjunct researcher at the University of Tasmania in Australia.

As you read, consider the following questions:

1. What percent of people displaced by extreme weather are women?
2. Which groups of women have a heightened risk of health issues related to climate change?
3. What does research indicate about the impact of gender diversity on a company's climate governance and sustainability practices?

When we think of climate and environmental issues such as climate-linked disasters or biodiversity loss, we don't tend to think about gender. At first glance, it may seem irrelevant.

But a growing body of evidence demonstrates women and gender-diverse people are disproportionately vulnerable to the changing climate and the consequences it brings.

Women are 14 times more likely to die in a climate change-related disaster than men. Women represent 80 percent of people displaced by extreme weather.

Although extreme weather events such as fires and floods might appear to affect everyone equally, the evidence shows crises exploit existing social faultlines. This means people who are already socially marginalised suffer exacerbated impacts.

What Does This Look Like?

Women are acutely impacted by environmental crises because they experience pre-existing social and economic disadvantage. Another reason is they tend to take responsibility for caring for other vulnerable groups, such as children or older people.

In a meta-analysis of 130 studies, 68 percent found women were more impacted by climate-linked health issues than men. Maternal and perinatal health is particularly affected by climate change hazards such as extreme heat. So too is the health of older women.

Most disturbingly, studies across Australia and around the world have revealed gender-based violence consistently increases during and after disasters. Both the most recent National Plan to End Violence against Women and Children and the associated Aboriginal and Torres Strait Islander Action Plan briefly recognise this. Even still, policymakers and service providers are yet to comprehensively grapple with what this means for women in an era of multiple and compounding disasters.

The impact of climate change on housing and living is also experienced in gendered ways. The Climate Council estimates that by 2030, 520,940 Australian properties, or one in every 25, will be "high-risk" and uninsurable. Rising costs of living, homelessness, and under-insured housing are all affecting Australian women, who are particularly vulnerable to losing food security and shelter.

Over 2016–21, men's homelessness increased by 1.6 percent while women's increased by just over 10 percent. The Australian housing crisis is being exacerbated by the climate crisis, and these impacts are distinctly gendered.

Leadership Drives Results

Research demonstrates women and gender-diverse people bring crucial perspectives and leadership to tackling these problems. They're not just helpless victims.

Evidence from across a range of sectors demonstrates gender-diverse leadership results in more effective and equitable approaches. Larger numbers of women in politics and policy-making results in stronger climate action policies, more ambitious climate targets, and more pro-environmental legislation. Despite this, at the COP28 climate talks in 2023, only 15 out of 140 speakers were women. Only 38 percent of party delegation members were women.

Gender diversity in industry leadership also yields environmental benefits. Research by the World Economic Forum shows that a 1 percent increase in women managers in a company results in a 0.5 percent decrease in carbon emissions. Boards with higher gender diversity receive higher scores on Environmental, Social, and Governance (ESG) performance measures and have fewer environmental lawsuits.

Companies with more than 30 percent, women on their boards display better climate governance, climate innovation and sustainability performance. Yet, as of 2022, women hold just one in four executive leadership positions in ASX300 companies. At the current rate of progress, it will take a century for women to constitute 40 percent of chief executives among ASX200 companies.

Women and gender-diverse people are also in the minority in renewable energy industries. Only around 35 percent of the clean energy workforce is female. These women are predominantly in jobs such as office administration, accounting, and cleaning, rather than trade-qualified or engineering roles.

In the recent federal budget, the government announced $55.6 million for a Building Women's Careers Program. It also pledged $38.2 million to increase diversity in Science, Technology, Engineering and Mathematics (STEM) education and industries. These are welcome developments.

But gender inclusion and equity need to be centred in major initiates like the Future Made in Australia Plan and the Net Zero Plan. This would help achieve urgent climate change mitigation targets and to ensure the associated economic benefits are genuinely inclusive.

Deep social change will be required to adequately address these issues. This is not just a matter of making space for more women to take up leadership positions, but requires grappling with the fact gendered social and economic inequality is caused by discriminatory gender attitudes, leaving women and gender-diverse people vulnerable to environmental impacts. Moreover, the kind of unpaid care work so often performed by women has been systematically undervalued, but is foundational to our economy, society, and environment.

Fuelling Disaster Recovery

Women also have a key role to play in preparing for and recovering from climate-fuelled disasters.

Research shows women tend to take on emotional and relational roles within communities, sustaining networks of care at the local level. Community-level care is crucial to helping local communities stay strong in the face of increasing disasters, the impacts of which often exceed the capacity of emergency responders. Our disaster response policies and agencies need to recognise the often gendered nature of community resilience work and deliberately support this kind of "soft infrastructure".

Climate and environmental issues do not affect us all equally. Women and gender-diverse people are acutely affected. We need targeted policy responses that recognise this vulnerability. In addition, women and gender-diverse people offer distinctive and much-needed leadership styles. These approaches are urgently required if we are to rapidly transition to a renewable economy.

The gendered impact of climate change is well-recognised at the international level, including by the United Nations. Australia has ambitions to host the COP31 global climate change conference with our Pacific neighbours in 2026. To be in the running, Australia needs to demonstrate it recognises and takes seriously the gendered nature of climate and environmental issues.

Periodical and Internet Sources Bibliography

The following articles have been selected to supplement the diverse views presented in this chapter.

Steve Baragona, "Five Ways Climate Change Is Making Poor People Poorer," *Voice of America*, May 25, 2022. https://www.voanews.com/a/five-ways-climate-change-is-making-poor-people-poorer/6583279.html.

Damian Carrington, "Children Set for More Climate Disasters Than Their Grandparents, Research Shows," the *Guardian*, September 26, 2021. https://www.theguardian.com/environment/2021/sep/27/children-set-for-more-climate-disasters-than-their-grandparents-research-shows.

Carmin Chappell, "Climate Change in the US Will Hurt Poor People the Most, According to a Bombshell Federal Report," CNBC, November 26, 2018. https://www.cnbc.com/2018/11/26/climate-change-will-hurt-poor-people-the-most-federal-report.html.

Darryl Fears and Dino Grandoni, "EPA Just Detailed all the Ways Climate Change Will Hit U.S. Racial Minorities the Hardest. It's a Long List," *Washington Post*, September 2, 2021. https://www.washingtonpost.com/climate-environment/2021/09/02/ida-climate-change/.

David Gelles and Mike Baker, "Judge Rules in Favor of Montana Youths in a Landmark Climate Case," *New York Times*, August 16, 2023. https://www.nytimes.com/2023/08/14/us/montana-youth-climate-ruling.html.

Mary Halton, "Climate change 'impacts women more than men,'" BBC, March 7, 2018. https://www.bbc.com/news/science-environment-43294221.

Mike Krings, "Marginalized communities develop 'disaster subculture' when living through extreme climate events, study finds," *University of Kansas News*, April 23, 2024. https://news.ku.edu/news/article/marginalized-communities-develop-disaster-subculture-when-living-through-extreme-climate-events-study-finds.

Joe McCarthy, "Why Climate Change and Poverty Are Inextricably Linked: Fighting One Problem Helps Mitigate the Other," Global

Citizen, February 19, 2020. https://www.globalcitizen.org/en/content/climate-change-is-connected-to-poverty/.

Giri Viswanathan, "Climate Change Can Have 'Lifelong Impacts' on Young People's Mental Health, Report Says," CNN, October 11, 2023. https://www.cnn.com/2023/10/11/health/climate-change-youth-mental-health/index.html.

Rachel Yavinsky, "Women More Vulnerable Than Men to Climate Change," Population Reference Bureau, December 26, 2012. https://www.prb.org/resources/women-more-vulnerable-than-men-to-climate-change/.

OPPOSING
VIEWPOINTS®
SERIES

CHAPTER 4

Do Corporations Often Engage in Greenwashing?

Chapter Preface

In the second chapter, the authors focused on the role of corporations in contributing to climate change and their responsibility for addressing the problem. And you've probably noticed that many of the companies you deal with got the memo. They promote many products and policies they claim are environmentally friendly or sustainable. But these claims often fall short of the truth.

When companies promote their business or their products as "green" when they are not, they are practicing "greenwashing." While no one argues against the fact that the practice is deceptive, it's not always clear what does and what does not constitute this sort of deception. For example, is it greenwashing when a company sets targets to reduce its carbon footprint yet does not meet those targets? Were the targets just for show, intended to make customers think they were doing something when they really weren't? Or were the company's targets just too ambitious?

In this chapter, the authors look at greenwashing from a variety of perspectives. The opening viewpoint argues that greenwashing does not require outright falsehoods. Deliberately misleading consumers through manipulative advertising amounts to the same thing.

Then subsequent viewpoints take a look at how marketing claims might actually benefit customers if customers could trust those claims. The second viewpoint argues for standardization in eco-labeling and sets forth a plan for how to do this. The following viewpoint looks at how corporations use deceptive marketing techniques to trick consumers into thinking they're more "green" than they actually are.

The author of the next viewpoint take a more philosophical approach to the problem, examining why consumers are willing to let corporations off the hook for greenwashing.

The fifth viewpoint focuses on the role sustainability reports written by external consultants play in greenwashing and why it's a problem.

> *"Overall, it's better that they're trying to do something than just ignoring the issue. But this is where you, the consumer, have to start doing your homework … and look for a provider that has a strong reputation and that is making claims validated by external sources."*

Greenwashing Doesn't Have to Be Overtly False to Be Deceptive

Tom Lyon

In this first viewpoint, SciLine interviews Tom Lyon about greenwashing and some of the "seven sins of greenwashing." These include the hidden tradeoff, in which a company claims it will do something good for the environment but fails to mention the bad things that go with it; irrelevance, in which a company is required by law to act in a certain environmentally conscious way instead of making the decision; and fibbing about what they are doing. He also discusses whether greenwashing is occurring in common practices like carbon offsets or planting a tree for every item sold, as well as how to find rating systems that can be trusted. While corporations should aim to make information about their sustainability practices more transparent and accessible, it is also the responsibility of consumers to help these efforst by doing their research and determining which corporations can be trusted. SciLine is a free service based at the nonprofit American Association for the Advancement of Science that helps journalists include scientific evidence and experts in their news stories. Tom Lyon is a professor of business economics and sustainable science, technology, and commerce at the University of Michigan.

As you read, consider the following questions:

1. According to Lyon, how common is the greenwashing sin of "fibbing"? Why is this the case?
2. Where do many carbon offsets come from? Is this effective at reducing emissions?
3. Which business practices referenced in this viewpoint do actually benefit the environment?

Many corporations claim their products are "green-friendly." But how do you know if what they're selling is truly eco-safe? SciLine interviewed Thomas Lyon, professor of sustainable science, technology, and commerce at the University of Michigan, on how to buy environmentally sustainable products, whether carbon credits actually work and the prevalence of greenwashing.

Below are some highlights from the discussion. Answers have been edited for brevity and clarity.

SciLine: What is greenwashing?

Thomas Lyon: Greenwashing is any communication that leads the listener to adopt an overly favorable impression of a company's greenness.

SciLine: How can the consumer avoid falling for it?

Thomas Lyon: I still love the old concept of the seven sins of greenwashing. The first and most common is what's called the sin of the hidden trade-off, where an organization tells you something good they do but neglects to tell you the bad things that go along with it.

For example, when you see an electric hand dryer in a public restroom, it may say on it: This dryer protects the environment. It saves trees from being used for paper.

But it neglects to tell you that, of course, it's powered with electricity, and that electricity may have been generated from coal-fired power, which might actually be more damaging than using a tree, which is a renewable resource. That's the most common of the seven deadly sins.

Other ones include the sin of irrelevance. For example, telling people that "this ship has an onboard wastewater recycling plant," when all ships that go to Alaska are required by law to have exactly that kind of equipment. It's no reflection of the company's quality.

The sin of fibbing is actually the least common. Companies don't usually actually lie about things. After all, it's against the law.

One of the increasingly common forms of greenwashing … is a hidden trade-off between the company's market activities and its political activities.

You may get a company that says: Look at this, we invested US$5 million in renewable energy last year. They may not tell you that they spent $100 billion drilling for oil in a sensitive location. And they may not tell you that they spent $50 million lobbying against climate legislation that would have made a real difference.

SciLine: What are carbon credits (or offsets)?

Thomas Lyon: I think the easiest way to understand these may be to step back a little bit and think about cap-and-trade systems… under which the government will set a cap on the aggregate amount of, say, carbon emissions. And within that, each company gets a right to emit a certain amount of carbon.

But that company can then trade permits with other companies. Suppose the company finds it's going to be really expensive for it to reduce its carbon emissions. But there's some other company next door that could do it really cheaply.

The company with the expensive reductions could pay the other company to do the reductions for it, and it then buys one of the permits—or more than one permit—from the company that can do it cheaply.

That kind of trading system has been recommended by economists for decades, because it lowers the overall cost of achieving a given level of emissions reduction. And that's a clean, well-enforced, reliable system.

Now the place where things get confusing for people is that a lot of times the offsets are not coming from within a cap-and-trade system. Instead they're coming from a voluntary offset that's offered by some free-standing producer that's not included in a cap.

Now it's necessary to ask a whole series of additional questions. Perhaps the foremost among them is: Is this offset actually producing a reduction that was not going to happen anyway?

It may be that the company claims, "Oh, we're saving this forest from being cut down." But maybe the forest was in a protected region in a country where there was no chance it was going to be cut down anyway. So that offset is not what is called in the offset world "additional."

SciLine: What should consumers make of companies that offer programs such as planting a tree for every widget they sell?

Thomas Lyon: Overall, it's better that they're trying to do something than just ignoring the issue. But this is where you, the consumer, have to start doing your homework … and look for a provider that has a strong reputation and that is making claims validated by external sources.

SciLine: Which rating schemes can people trust?

Thomas Lyon: There's a cool little app that I like a lot. You can download it. It's called EWG Healthy Living. EWG stands for Environmental Working Group. It's a group of scientists who get together and draw on science to assess which products are environmentally friendly, and which ones aren't. And they have something like 150,000 products in their database.

You can scan the UPC code when you go to the store, and you just immediately get this information up on your phone that rates the quality of the company's environmental claims and performance. That's a really nice little way to verify things on the fly.

SciLine: Are there any examples of business practices that really do benefit the environment?

Thomas Lyon: Building is one big area. LEED building standards or Energy Star building standards reduce environmental impact. They improve the quality of the indoor environment for employees. They actually produce higher rents because people are more willing to work in these kinds of buildings.

You can look at the whole movement toward renewable energy and companies that produce solar or wind energy. They're doing something that really is good for the environment.

The move toward electric vehicles—that really will be good for the environment. It does raise trade-offs. There are going to be issues around certain critical mineral inputs into producing batteries, and we've got to figure out good ways to reuse batteries and then dispose of them at the end of their life.

> *"Currently, there is no consistent benchmark for the development of eco-labels which presents a risk of misinformation, consumer confusion, and the potential for 'greenwashing'."*

Eco-Labels Must Be Standardized

The British Standards Institution

Greenwashing is deceitful as well as bad for business, according to the previous viewpoint. However, honest information about the sustainability of products can be useful. Here, the British Standards Institution explains what eco-labeling is and why it is needed. It also argues for the necessity of standardizing eco-labeling, as this will allow greater consistency and transparency in how these companies act. The British Standards Institution (BSI) is the national standards body of the United Kingdom. It produces technical standards on a wide range of products and services and supplies certifications.

As you read, consider the following questions:

1. How do food systems impact the environment, according to this viewpoint?
2. What is eco-labeling?
3. Why is standardization crucial for eco-labeling to work?

Many consumers underestimate the impact of the food supply chain on climate change, but the reality is that food systems account for around 21 to 37 percent of global greenhouse gas emissions according to the Intergovernmental Panel on Climate Change (IPCC), whilst agriculture is the world's leading driver of deforestation. To help address these challenges, eco-labeling seeks to give consumers better information about the environmental credentials of products, supporting consumers to make more sustainable choices during their food shop.

Currently, with limited eco-labeling, consumers can find it challenging to make more sustainable purchases despite the fact that 65 percent of consumers want to make the right choices to live a healthier and more sustainable lifestyle, as recently reported by the World Economic Forum. Set against the backdrop of rising ethical consumerism which is now valued at £122 billion according to the 2021 Co-op Ethical Consumerism Report, consumers are looking for messaging that is easy to recognize, connect with, and understand.

With the European Parliament recently adopting proposals which will require companies to ensure the reliability and accuracy of their voluntary environmental claims, this begs the question: what role could eco-labeling play in improving consumer confidence in the sustainability of food products?

The Use of Eco-Labeling for More Sustainable Production and Consumption

Eco-labels are voluntarily placed on products by brands to help consumers make informed purchasing decisions by providing information about the sustainability of a product.

Research by the British Psychological Society has shown that eco-labeling on menus encourages people to eat more sustainably, with more people (84 percent) opting for the more sustainable choices in the eco-label study, compared with the control study (69 percent). Similarly, the application of Nutri-Score labels to products in French supermarkets apply the principles of nudge theory to encourage consumers to choose more nutritional products. The success of the Nutri-Score System has led to the initiative being recommended for use in other European Union countries, as well as by the European Commission and the World Health Organization.

Eco-labeling could achieve comparable results for raising consumer awareness of the carbon footprint of food products and drive rapid improvements in sustainability throughout the food supply chain, whilst also removing some confusion for consumers about how to make the best eco-friendly choices.

As more sustainable products often carry a price premium which could discourage consumers if they are not aware of the product's sustainability credentials, eco-labels have an important role to play in supporting consumers to make more sustainable choices.

The charity Foundation Earth have been working with brands and retailers including Nestle and M&S to run successful eco-labelling trials. The trials were welcomed by the UK government, which recognized the potential of the labels to help address the urgent challenges of sustainability and climate change.

The Need for Standardized Eco-Labels and the Role of Standards in Providing More Consistency and Transparency

With reported incidents of "greenwashing" contributing to skepticism among consumers about eco-friendly claims, it is important that sustainability information presented to consumers is genuinely meaningful and truthful. Oatly's adverts comparing their plant-based products to dairy milk were banned by the Advertising Standards Authority or misleading claims about carbon emissions, for instance, illustrating that producers and brands must ensure authenticity about sustainability claims to gain the trust of an increasingly environmentally conscious market.

Currently, there is a lack of agreed standards for eco-labeling of food. Despite this, some food brands and retailers are already starting to adopt their own eco-labeling practices without the

CONSUMERS MUST BE
INFORMED AND ENGAGED

As consumers, we have the power to choose what we buy, and this power comes with the responsibility to choose wisely. Similarly, corporations have the responsibility to produce products that are safe, ethical, and sustainable, while also providing consumers with the freedom to choose what they want to buy.

[...] Many consumers are becoming more aware of the environmental and social impact of fast fashion and are choosing to buy from companies that prioritise sustainability and ethical production practices. For example, Patagonia is a company that has built its brand around sustainability and has made a commitment to using environmentally friendly materials and manufacturing processes. By providing consumers with the option to buy sustainably produced clothing, Patagonia is empowering consumers to make choices that are better for the environment.

Another example of consumer freedom and corporate responsibility is the trend of companies offering plant-based food options. As more consumers adopt plant-based diets for health and environmental reasons, companies like Beyond Meat and Impossible Foods have emerged to meet this demand. By offering plant-based alternatives to meat, these companies are giving consumers the freedom to choose what they want to eat, while also reducing the environmental impact of meat production.

However, consumer freedom and corporate responsibility are not always aligned. In some cases, corporations prioritise their own profits over the well-being of consumers. One example of this is the food industry's use of artificial additives and preservatives. While these additives may make food cheaper and more convenient to produce, they can have negative health effects on consumers. For example, the preservative BHA has been linked to cancer in animal studies, yet it is still used in many processed foods. By prioritizing profits over consumer health, corporations are failing in their responsibility to produce safe and ethical products.

[...]

To ensure that consumer freedom and corporate responsibility are aligned, it is important for consumers to be informed and engaged. By educating themselves on the environmental and social impact

> of the products they buy, consumers can make more informed choices and hold corporations accountable for their actions. Similarly, by supporting companies that prioritise sustainability, ethics, and transparency, consumers can send a message that these values are important.
>
> [...]
>
> "Consumer Freedom and Corporate Responsibility: Striking a Balance" by Yash Mishra. Insights, May 12, 2023.

guidance of an industry standard. This means that, currently, there is no consistent benchmark for the development of eco-labels which presents a risk of misinformation, consumer confusion, and the potential for "greenwashing"

By providing consistency and transparency to eco-labeling through an industry standard, the risk of misinformation and confusion when purchasing food would be reduced whilst giving consumers more confidence in the sustainability claims of food brands. A new standard would also encourage businesses to ensure sustainable production systems and invest in innovative, carbon-neutral technologies to ensure that they can display the highest eco-label rating on their products.

Developing a standard for eco-labeling to give consumers an easy way to make evidence-based purchasing decisions about the environmental impact of their diet requires collaboration between business, academia, and government throughout the standard development, to ensure that the labels can be clearly and accurately understood by consumers.

BSI as a Facilitator for Sustainable Change in the Food Industry

At BSI, we have proven success of engaging with industries, businesses and governments to create consensus-based standards that define what "good" looks like. We have extensive research and intelligence capabilities, with a track record of driving change in the food industry through collaborative work with various organizations.

We've created standards that address the food industry's shifting landscape and support initiatives which positively impact our planet and people. For example, our guide to responsible innovation (PAS 440) has been implemented by biotechnology startup MiAlgae. MiAlgae produce omega-3-rich algae using co-products from the whisky industry, thus addressing food waste and providing an omega-3 source that doesn't rely on depleting fish stocks.

Our collaboration with the food industry has also led to fast-track standards such as the guide to protecting and defending food and drink from deliberate attack (PAS 96) and a new document on the criteria to define 100 percent plant-based foods (PAS 224).

By developing effective standards, BSI plays an essential role in helping businesses, organizations and government achieve net zero targets and become more transparent through better monitoring and reporting.

BSI can also support the food industry to build resilience, transform, and grow through expert strategy, research and intelligence, standards landscaping, standards creation, advisory services, gap analysis, and implementation support.

> *"The widespread use of these claims could delay important action on tackling climate change, as it dilutes the sense of urgency around the issue."*

Companies Use Deceitful Marketing Techniques to Make Consumers Think They're Green

Christine Parker

In this viewpoint Christine Parker discusses the prevalence of ads for businesses and products claiming to be "green" on social media. She discusses a study that she and her colleagues conducted on Facebook ads, which concluded that many green claims are inaccurate or unsubstantiated. Language indicating that something is "sustainable," "eco-friendly," "clean," and "carbon neutral" tends to lack data to back it up. Nature imagery and symbols like a leaf, the green checkmark, Earth, or a recycling symbol also signal to consumers that a product or company is ecofriendly, but again, there is little to substantiate these claims. Parker argues that governments need to create laws to create standards for "green" claims in advertising and clarify what these terms mean. Christine Parker is a professor of law at the University of Melbourne in Australia.

"Social Media Ads Are Littered with 'Green' Claims. How Are We Supposed to Know They're True?," by Christine Parker, The Conversation, November 30, 2023, https://theconversation.com/social-media-ads-are-littered-with-green-claims-how-are-we-supposed-to-know-theyre-true-218922. Licensed under CC BY-ND 4.0 International.

As you read, consider the following questions:

1. What colors are used to make a product or business seem ecofriendly?
2. What are the top five sectors that make green claims?
3. What is the European Union attempting to do to prevent misleading environmental claims?

Online platforms are awash with ads for so-called "green" products. Power companies are "carbon neutral." Electronics are "for the planet." Clothing is "circular," and travel is "sustainable." Or are they?

Our study of more than 8,000 ads served more than 20,000 times in people's Facebook feeds found many green claims are vague, meaningless, or unsubstantiated and consumers are potentially being deceived.

This costs consumers, as products claiming to be greener are often more expensive. And it costs the planet, as false and exaggerated green claims – or "greenwashing" – make it seem more is being done to tackle climate change and other environmental crises than is really happening.

The widespread use of these claims could delay important action on tackling climate change, as it dilutes the sense of urgency around the issue.

The Colours of Environmental Friendliness

Our research is part of a newly published report produced by the not-for-profit Consumer Policy Research Centre, researchers at Melbourne Law School and the Australian Ad Observatory, a project of ADM+S (ARC Centre of Excellence for Automated Decision-Making and Society).

The Ad Observatory captures ads from the personal Facebook feeds of around 2,000 people who "donate" their ads to the project via a browser plugin. This lets us analyse otherwise unobservable and ephemeral ads.

We found the most common claims were "clean," "green," and "sustainable." Other popular terms were "bio," "recycled" or "recyclable," "pure," and "eco-friendly," often with no explanation of what lay behind them. All are very general, undefined terms, yet they imply a more environmentally responsible choice.

Our report didn't verify each claim nor analysed their accuracy. We intended to highlight the volume and breadth of the green claims consumers see in social media ads.

Many ads used colors and symbols to put a green "halo" around their products and business. These included green, blue, and earthy beige tones, background nature imagery, and emojis featuring leaves, planet Earth, the recycling symbol, and the green tick, often with no context or specific information.

The top five sectors making green claims were energy, household products, fashion, health and personal care, and travel.

This was consistent with a recent internet sweep by the Australian Competition and Consumer Commission (ACCC), which found 57 percent of the business websites checked were making concerning claims. The proportion was highest among the cosmetic, clothing and footwear, and food and drink packaging sectors.

Strong Incentives for Greenwashing

Recent Consumer Policy Research Centre research shows 45 percent percent of Australians always or often consider sustainability as part of their purchasing decision-making. At least 50 percent of Australians say they are worried about green claim truthfulness across every sector.

Given consumer concern, businesses have a strong incentive to "green" their businesses. But that comes with a strong incentive to claim more than is justified.

Major Australian business regulators—the ACCC and Australian Securities and Investment Commission (ASIC)—are both prioritising enforcement action against greenwashing.

ASIC has issued dozens of interventions against misleading and deceptive environmental disclosures by companies and super funds. The ACCC has issued draft guidance for businesses on how to avoid greenwashing when making environmental and sustainability claims.

A Senate inquiry into greenwashing is expected to report in mid-2024 as to whether stricter regulation is necessary to protect consumers from misleading greenwashing.

What Is "Sustainable," Anyway?

Our research highlights the plethora of green claims businesses make in social media advertising. Consumers are forced to choose between accepting claims at face value or committing to a deep dive to research each product they buy and the claims they make.

Many green claims come from the energy sector, with some energy companies claiming to be "greener" without any detail. Some claim carbon offsets or carbon neutrality – highly contested terms.

Ads for "sustainable" travel often showed destinations emphasising a connection with nature but did not explain what aspect of the travel was sustainable.

One personal care brand heavily advertised its "sustainable" packaging, but the fine print showed it related only to the boxes their products are shipped in, not the actual product packaging. A claim like this can create an undeserved green halo across a whole product range.

Claims that products are biodegradable, compostable or recyclable can be particularly problematic, since this is often technically true yet practically difficult. Some products labeled biodegradable may need to be taken to a specific facility, but a consumer might assume they will biodegrade in their home compost bin.

What Can We Do?

Australians cannot wait years for enforcement action against potentially misleading green claims. The economy and the digital world is moving too fast and the need for sustainability is too urgent. Governments must enact laws now to ensure green terms are clearly defined and based on the truth.

The European Union is currently working on a "Green claims" directive that seeks to ban generic claims such as "eco-friendly," "green," "carbon positive," and "energy efficient". Claims would have to be specific, meaningful, and based on independently verified excellent environmental performance.

The United Kingdom has already issued similar guidance via an environmental claims code and is also considering stricter legislation.

Australian regulators should have the power to blacklist green terms that cannot be substantiated and are inherently meaningless or misleading.

Some high-polluting sectors should be banned from making any kind of green claim in advertising, due to the overwhelming negative environmental impact of their business models and practices, as the EU is considering. Fossil-fuel companies, for example, should not be permitted to use green claims in marketing.

Australian consumers deserve green choices that are clear, comparable, meaningful and true.

> *"Results showed that greenwashing took much less of a toll on the perceived trustworthiness of the oil and gas company. As a result, consumers said they were significantly more likely to purchase its products and services."*

Consumers Often Give Polluting Companies a Pass for Greenwashing

Adam Austen Kay

In this viewpoint Adam Austen Kay examines a study he and his colleagues conducted on how consumers respond to greenwashers in "dirty" industries like oil and gas. They found that if an industry is already stigmatized for not being ecofriendly, consumers care less if companies in these industries are found to be greenwashing. These companies are held to a much lower standard than companies in "clean" or "neutral" industries. While "clean" or "neutral" companies that are found to be greenwashing tend to suffer a significant negative financial impact, "dirty" companies do not, which incentivizes them to continue their harmful and dishonest practices. Adam Austen Kay is a lecturer in the School of Business at the University of Queensland in Australia.

As you read, consider the following questions:

1. Among the companies studied, which types of companies were not penalized for greenwashing?
2. How does a "boys will be boys" attitude apply to attitudes toward greenwashing?
3. According to Kay, why does the issue of letting polluters off the hook for greenwashing matter on a broader societal scale?

Stigma is an awful burden for business. But what if—for some companies—stigma is an asset?

That's what I and an international team of researchers set out to investigate in a new paper published in the *Journal of Management Studies.*

We examined how consumers around the world responded to firms in stigmatised industries like oil and gas that are found "greenwashing," meaning they claim to do more for the environment than they really do.

We anticipated that the market would punish greenwashers, but we thought it would treat firms seen to be "dirty" rather differently.

Specifically, we thought the market would either

- punish dirty firms *more*, as might the judge of a repeat offender in court; or
- punish dirty firms *less*, as might parents who overlook poor behavior by their child with outdated excuses like "boys will be boys".

What we discovered has important implications for greenwashing and important implications more broadly.

What We Found

In a study tracking 7,365 companies in 47 countries over 15 years, we found that consumers financially penalised firms for greenwashing—but not if those firms were stigmatised as dirty.

In other words, the market imposed a kind of tax on companies for greenwashing, unless they were already regarded as big polluters.

In order to find out why stigmatised greenwashers were exempt from this market tax, we conducted a follow-up experiment.

After a pre-study to determine which industries are most regarded as "dirty," "clean," or "neutral" (the answers were oil and gas, solar and wind power, and stationery and office supplies), we presented 458 consumers with a statement from the corporate citizenship report of a firm in one of these three industries.

In the statement, the firm professed its core values of honesty, integrity, and environmental sustainability. The only difference between the three versions of the statement was the industry the firm was in.

> We at [Company X] take environmental sustainability very seriously. We understand that, as a business that relies on natural resources, if we do not manage those resources carefully today then our business tomorrow will be in jeopardy. For this reason, we make environmental sustainability central to virtually every aspect of our business. Indeed, we pride ourselves as an industry leader when it comes to environmental practices. Ultimately, anything less would not only be a disservice to our planet, but also to our stakeholders.

Next, we presented consumers the results of an independent environmental audit that either found the firm to be acting in line with its professed values or not (i.e., greenwashing).

> …However, contrary to what [Company X] states, recent results of an independent third-party environmental audit suggest that [Company X] is not as concerned with environmental sustainability as it says it is. For example, [Company X] was found not to do anything to reduce the environmental impact of its products, such as sourcing local or recycled materials for production and packaging. In addition, last year [Company X] released 7.8 million gallons of chemical byproducts from its factories into rivers and streams, instead of disposing of them in an environmentally responsible manner (as it could have

done). Moreover, rather than taking steps to address climate change, last year [Company X] actually increased its carbon footprint by a whopping 20 percent.

Results showed that greenwashing took much less of a toll on the perceived trustworthiness of the oil and gas company. As a result, consumers said they were significantly more likely to purchase its products and services.

Taken together, these two studies suggest that consumers have a "boys will be boys" attitude to greenwashing by dirty firms. They even expect it.

Why This Matters for Greenwashing

Our findings have important implications for how to regulate greenwashing.

First, it's often assumed that consumers punish greenwashers, but data supporting this assumption is hard to come by. We demonstrate empirically that this assumption is true. For many firms, greenwashing results in real financial costs.

Second, we find the market penalty for greenwashing is much weaker for firms that are regarded as dirty. Those who expect the market to punish greenwashing by firms in the oil and gas industry and other heavy polluters should reconsider.

Third, our findings suggest governments and international organisations that have a "zero tolerance" approach to greenwashing should focus their limited resources on dirty industries and let the market take care of the rest.

Why This Matters More Broadly

The "boys will be boys" attitude that we uncovered in this research is likely to play out in other fields in which people respond to the misdeeds of "bad boys", including politics.

An example might be former US President Donald Trump. Having survived scandal after scandal, Trump once famously declared that he could shoot someone on Fifth Avenue and not lose votes.

The more deplorable the media has made him out to be—the greater the stigma attached to the Trump name—the less his misdeeds seem to have hurt him. Our research offers new clues as to why.

As consumers and voters, we need to recognise that our "boys will be boys" attitude enables bad behavior. Unless we do, and until we regulate with this psychological bias in mind, we will continue to be part of the problem.

> *"Companies publish these reports as their own documents. But often, externally hired consultants play an invisible role in gathering data and framing it in a positive narrative the public will find easy to digest."*

Sustainability Reports Often Facilitate Greenwashing

Hendri Yulius Wijaya and Kate Macdonald

In this viewpoint Hendri Yulius Wijaya and Kate Macdonald examine companies' use of environmental, social, and governance (ESG) reports and the role independent consultants play in this process. The authors explain that although some countries require reporting from companies, in others it is voluntary, but many companies still choose to engage in it. In theory, the consulting firms that create the reports are supposed to be dedicated to sustainable business practices and offering their assessments in an unbiased way, but in reality, they try to put a positive spin on companies' activities to make them seem more ecofriendly than they actually are in order for the consulting firms to stay in business. Changes must be made to the reporting process to ensure consumers are getting accurate information. At the time this viewpoint was published, Hendri Yulius Wijaya was a PhD student in political science at the University of Melbourne in Australia, where Kate Macdonald is an associate professor of political science.

As you read, consider the following questions:

1. What are environmental, social, and governance (ESG) reports?
2. How do consulting firms legitimize their expertise?
3. What changes to ESG reporting do the authors believe would help?

Around the world, more and more companies are publishing sustainability reports – public scorecards detailing their impacts on society and the environment.

Environmental, social and governance (ESG) reports outline the positive and negative effects of a company's activities, and the steps they're taking in response.

Companies publish these reports as their own documents. But often, externally hired consultants play an invisible role in gathering data and framing it in a positive narrative the public will find easy to digest.

And getting these reports independently evaluated—"external assurance"—is still not required by many regulators around the world. As a result, they can allow companies to "greenwash".

This could be by only disclosing information that makes a company look "sustainable" to the public. Or by only reporting on categories that paint them in a good light, and excluding the less flattering ones.

The problems inherent in this process create a blind spot for society. We urgently need to shine a light on consultants' unseen involvement in sustainability reporting.

The Business of Polishing 'Facts'

It's increasingly becoming mandatory for large publicly traded companies to disclose their social and environmental performance, particularly across Europe and the Asia-Pacific region.

In Australia, such reporting is voluntary, but widespread. As many as 98 percent of top Australian companies published sustainability reports last year. Consulting firms have quickly expanded their existing lines of service to capture this growing market opportunity.

Consultancies legitimise their expertise by offering businesses a range of frameworks and discourses. These convey the benefits of implementing sustainability measures and show how they could boost profitability.

But use of the firms has attracted heavy criticism.

One argument is that consulting firms actually undermine their own sustainability services by continuing to do work for major companies in polluting industries, such as the oil and gas sector.

Another is that consulting firms' contributions to sustainability are largely superficial. It's too easy for companies to engage them just to tick boxes—perhaps to meet certain global standards or frameworks in bad faith, or create the impression they are responsible companies in other ways.

Problems with the Process

Drawing on the lead author's previous experience as a sustainability reporting professional in Indonesia, we wanted to take a closer look at these criticisms.

To examine the issue properly, we need to recognise that a power imbalance can arise between external consultants and the companies that hire them when sustainability reports are treated as an end in themselves or "time-bound projects".

This attitude stands in stark contrast to the continuous strategy of measurement and disclosure that is required to create meaningful change at a company.

First, with such a narrow view of reporting, consultants are treated as simply a service provider—they are hired to complete a report within a given timeframe. But this limits their exposure to a company's overall operations. Consultants have to rely on information passed on to them by employees, or they distribute oversimplified, generic forms for the organisation's members to quickly fill in.

Who they get to speak with to gather this information is also completely at the whim of their client. Under these constraints and tight deadlines, it's difficult for them to perform meaningful data analysis.

Second, in practice, "reporting" often actually means "selecting which information shall and shall not be presented to the public".

Using external consultants to prepare a report might seem like it would offer an unbiased or independent perspective. But the reports are heavily scrutinised by company management, who ultimately make the final decision about what to include.

And third, pressure to comply with certain regulations and standards can make companies shortsighted. Consultants are tasked with ensuring a company "ticks the box" and fulfils its reporting requirements. But if this is the primary incentive, the information presented can be superficial and lack context.

A deeper contextual analysis is necessary to describe what lies behind the raw numbers, including a company's challenges, improvement targets and the path forward.

What Needs to Change?

Consultants can still play a key role in the global move to ESG reporting. But the industry's approach needs to change.

For one, sustainability reports cover a wide range of ESG topics—from climate to social inclusion. It is impossible for a single consultant to tackle all of them simultaneously. Companies should ensure there is a diverse range of experts in the teams they hire.

More countries could also pass laws requiring "external assurance"—independent, standardised cross checking of companies' sustainability reports.

Meanwhile, companies and consultants need to return to the underlying principle of sustainability reporting: it's not just about producing marketing material. Faced with a very real global crisis, it's a key way to measure the impacts, risks, and challenges of doing business, and present a company's action plan to address them.

It's important to be sceptical when the information in a sustainability report only shows good performance. Nobody is perfect. Neither is any business.

Periodical and Internet Sources Bibliography

The following articles have been selected to supplement the diverse views presented in this chapter.

Daniel Ackerman and Meghna Chakrabarti, "How Big Oil helped push the idea of a 'carbon footprint,'" WBUR, December 19, 2023. https://www.wbur.org/onpoint/2023/12/19/how-big-oil-helped-push-the-idea-of-a-carbon-footprint.

Jake Bolster, "The Quest to Make Big Oil Pay for Climate Change," *New Lines*, January 1, 2024. https://newlinesmag.com/reportage/the-quest-to-make-big-oil-pay-for-climate-change/.

Jason Bordoff, "Behind All the Talk, This Is What Big Oil Is Actually Doing," *New York Times*, August 7, 2023. https://www.nytimes.com/2023/08/07/opinion/oil-fossil-fuels-clean-energy.html.

Peter Eavis and Clifford Krauss, "What's Really Behind Corporate Promises on Climate Change?" *New York Times*, February 22, 2021. https://www.nytimes.com/2021/02/22/business/energy-environment/corporations-climate-change.html.

Chris McGreal, "Big Oil and Gas Kept a Dirty Secret for Decades. Now They May Pay the Price," the *Guardian*, June 30, 2021. https://www.theguardian.com/environment/2021/jun/30/climate-crimes-oil-and-gas-environment.

Katie Myers, "These Four States Want Big Oil to Pay for Climate Damage," *Mother Jones*, February 12, 2024. https://www.motherjones.com/politics/2024/02/climate-change-superfund-legislation-compensation-flooding-adaptation-costs/.

Maud Sarliève, "Climate Change: How to Make Corporations Responsible," JusticeInfo, December 5, 2019. https://www.justiceinfo.net/en/43130-climate-change-how-to-make-corporations-responsible.html.

Kristin Toussaint, "If 100 Companies Are Responsible for 70% of Emissions, What Can You Do?" *Fast Company*, October 13, 2021. https://www.fastcompany.com/90680284/heres-how-to-push-for-action-on-the-climate-crisis.

Jeff Wilser, "How Small Businesses Can Have a Big Impact in the Climate Fight," *Time*, October 13, 2022. https://time.com/6213434/climate-change-action-companies-businesses/.

For Further Discussion

Chapter 1

1. Various authors in this chapter assert that addressing climate change will take international cooperation. Can you think of examples when nations worked together to solve a problem that affected them all? Can you think of examples where a lack of international cooperation made, or continues to make, a problem worse?
2. After reading the viewpoints in this chapter, how do you think the inequities of climate change should be addressed among nations?
3. What do you think is the responsibility of major CO_2-emitting nations to stop curb emissions and prevent climate change?

Chapter 2

1. The authors of the first viewpoint in this chapter point out that one's views about capitalism and a free-market economy can influence views about climate policy, even when a person knows that climate change is real. Why do you think a person might maintain this ideological position even when the facts show it to be dangerous?
2. Authors in this chapter touch on the debate about Big Oil trying to shift the blame for climate change onto consumers, who are the end users of their product. On the other hand, oil companies have been caught lying to the public about climate change and have refused to take steps to mitigate the damage caused by their products. Who do you think is most to blame, and who should bear most of the burden of solving this problem?
3. Developed nations built their economies on fossil fuels. Do developing nations have the right to do the same thing, to put the growth of their economies ahead of the health of

the planet and those who live on it? If not, can you think of fair solutions that would protect developing nations' economic development while at the same time addressing climate change?

Chapter 3

1. People who are young today will bear greater hardships from climate change than those who are older now. Do you think young people should have a greater voice in climate policy? If so, how should young people make sure their voices are heard?
2. Climate change is already hitting harder in marginalized communities, yet the excessive use of fossil fuels that created the problem is due mostly to the activities of wealthier communities. What, if anything, do you think rich nations and rich communities owe to the poor?
3. Based on what you've read in this chapter, how are girls, women, and gender-diverse people impacted by climate change? What can be done to help address these impacts?

Chapter 4

1. Greenwashing, even when it's just misleading rather than outright lying, is deceiving the public about important matters. Can you think of ways the public can make it clear to companies they do business with that they want those companies to be honest with them? Do you think consumers can have an impact?
2. In this chapter, we learn that many companies voluntarily report their emissions and other environmentally impactful activities, yet greenwashing still occurs. Why is this the case, and what can be done to ensure more honest and complete reporting?
3. What are some marketing methods companies use to greenwash their products and businesses? What can consumers do to avoid being tricked by misleading advertising?

Organizations to Contact

The editors have compiled the following list of organizations concerned with the issues debated in this book. The descriptions are derived from materials provided by the organizations. All have publications or information available for interested readers. The list was compiled on the date of publication of the present volume; the information provided here may change. Be aware that many organizations take several weeks or longer to respond to inquiries, so allow as much time as possible.

350.org
20 Jay Street
Suite 732
Brooklyn, NY 11201
email: Natalia@350.org
website: https://350.org

As a non-profit organization, 350.org is focused on building a global climate movement through grassroots organizing and mass public actions. It aims to reduce the use of fossil fuels and increase the use of renewable energy sources.

Alliance for Climate Education
4696 Broadway
Suite 2
Boulder, CO 80304
(702) 526-2231
email: hello@acespace.org
website: https://acespace.org

The Alliance for Climate Education is an organization that educates students about climate change and empowers them to lead on climate solutions. It has a youth action network that allows young people to join together and advocate for climate justice.

Center for Sustainable Energy

3980 Sherman Street, Suite 170
San Diego, CA 92110
(858) 244-1177
website: https://energycenter.org

An independent non-profit organization, the Center for Sustainable Energy is working to use software-enabled program design, administration, and services to transform markets for clean transportation and distributed energy. It works with governments, utilities, and the private sector to accelerate the adoption of clean energy.

Christians for Social Action (CSA)

1300 Eagle Road
St. Davids, PA 19087
Email: CSA@eastern.edu
website: https://christiansforsocialaction.org

CSA is a group of Christian scholar-activists aiming to stir the imagination for a fuller expression of Christian faithfulness and a more just society, including environmental justice. It is a part of the Sider Center of Eastern University in St. Davids, Pennsylvania.

Climate Justice Alliance

(202) 455-8665
email: Info@ClimateJusticeAlliance.org
https://climatejusticealliance.org

Climate Justice Alliance is a united group of communities and organizations that believe the process of transitioning from extractive systems of production, consumption, and political oppression toward resilient, regenerative, and equitable economies must place race, gender, and class at the center of the solutions. It works to accomplish these goals at a local level while also creating interlinked strategies across the country.

Climate Reality Project

555 11th Street NW
Suite 601
Washington, DC 20004
website: www.climaterealityproject.org

The Climate Reality Project recruits, trains, and mobilizes people to take climate action. It was founded by former U.S. Vice President Al Gore and works to encourage urgent global action in support of climate justice and clean energy.

Corporate Accountability

(617) 695-2525
website: http://corporateaccountability.org

This organization works to stop transnational organizations from devastating democracy, the environment, and human rights and create a world where corporations answer to people, not the other way around. It launches strategic campaigns to compel governments and transnational corporations to stop harming health, the environment, human rights, and democracy.

David Suzuki Foundation

219-2211 West 4th Ave.
Vancouver, BC V6K 4S2
(604) 732-4228
website: www.davidsuzuki.org

The David Suzuki Foundation is an organization that collaborates with Canadians from all walks of life—including government and business—to preserve the environment and create a sustainable Canada. It offers suggestions for how individuals can take climate action online and within their local communities.

Green America

1612 K Street NW, Suite 1,000
Washington, DC 20006
(800) 584-7336
website: https://greenamerica.org

Green America uses the economic power of consumers, investors, businesses, and the marketplace to help create a more socially just and environmentally sustainable society. It connects climate issues to finance, food systems, labor, and social justice issues to support a healthy planet and society.

Oxfam America

1101 17th St NW, Suite 1300
Washington, DC 20036
(800) 776-9326
email: info@oxfamamerica.org
website: www.oxfamamerica.org

Oxfam America is an international organization that fights inequality to end poverty and injustice. It advocates for economic justice, gender equality, and climate action.

Zero Hour

email: info@thisiszerohour.org
website: https://thisiszerohour.org

Zero Hour is a youth-led movement offering training and resources for a new generation of climate-change activists who want to take concrete action against climate change. Its goal is to protect the rights of the next generation to a clean, safe, and healthy environment.

Bibliography of Books

John Freeman, ed. *Tales of Two Planets: Stories of Climate Change and Inequality in a Divided World.* New York, NY: Penguin, 2020.

Saul Griffith. *Electrify: An Optimist's Playbook for Our Clean Energy Century.* Cambridge, MA: MIT Press, 2021.

Avery Elizabeth Hurt. *A Global Threat: The Emergence of Climate Change Science.* New York, NY: Cavendish Square, 2017.

Hope Jahren. *The Story of More: How We Got to Climate Change and Where We Go from Here.* New York, NY: Penguin, 2020.

Ayana Elizabeth Johnson and Katharine K. Wilkinson, eds. *All We Can Save: Truth, Courage, and Solutions for the Climate Crisis.* New York, NY: One World, 2021.

Naomi Klein. *How to Change Everything: The Young Human's Guide to Protecting the Planet and Each Other.* New York, NY: Atheneum Books for Young Readers, 2021.

Naomi Klein. *This Changes Everything: Capitalism versus the Climate.* New York, NY: Simon and Schuster, 2014.

Elizabeth Kolbert. *Field Notes from a Catastrophe: Man, Nature, and Climate Change.* Reprint ed. New York, NY: Bloomsbury, 2015.

Elizabeth Kolbert. *H Is for Hope: Climate Change from A to Z.* Berkeley, CA: Ten Speed Press, 2023.

Naomi Oreskes and Erik M. Conway. *The Big Myth: How American Business Taught Us to Loathe Government and Love the Free Market.* New York, NY: Bloomsbury, 2023.

Naomi Oreskes and Erik M. Conway. *Merchants of Doubt: How a Handful of Scientists Obscured the Truth on Issues from Tobacco Smoke to Climate Change.* New York, NY: Bloomsbury, 2010.

Nathaniel Rich. *Losing Earth: A Recent History*. New York, NY: Farrar, Straus and Giroux, 2019.

Mary Robinson. *Climate Justice: Hope, Resilience, and the Fight for a Sustainable Future*. New York, NY: Bloomsbury, 2019.

Rebecca Solnit and Thelma Young Lutunatabua, eds. *Not Too Late: Changing the Climate Story from Despair to Possibility*. Chicago, IL: Haymarket, 2023.

Greta Thunberg. *The Climate Book: The Facts and the Solutions*. New York, NY: Penguin, 2023.

Index

A

Africa, 22, 42, 45, 47, 76, 84–102, 104–105

agriculture, crops, and agricultural work, 15, 22, 27–28, 39–40, 47–48, 51, 59, 76, 104, 111, 121, 124, 144

Antigua and Barbuda, 31

Asia, 47, 115, 161

Australia, 51, 76, 129–131, 160–161

B

Bangladesh, 53

Barbados, 26, 30

Belarus, 53

Bhutan, 30, 95

biodiversity, 32–36, 52, 128

Bolivia, 53

C

Cambodia, 53

Canada, 54

capitalism, 67–69, 90–93, 96–97

carbon and carbon issues, 15, 18, 29, 32–37, 44, 46, 56–58, 63, 67, 74–76, 78, 81, 84, 86–87, 98, 109–110, 112–113, 121, 130, 136–138, 140, 145, 147, 149, 152, 157

"carbon billionaires," 74–75, 78

China, 29, 53, 56–57, 60–62, 76, 86, 110

coal, 39–40, 58, 62, 85–87, 122, 139

corporations and companies, 15–16, 30, 36–37, 39–41, 63, 65, 67–85, 90–98, 106, 121, 136–163

Costa Rica, 53

COVID-19 pandemic, 29, 119, 121

D

Dominica, 27

drought, 25–26, 44–46, 56, 59, 88, 102–104, 109, 111, 120–121, 125

E

eco-labeling, 136, 143–145, 147–149

Egypt, 20–24, 45, 53, 60, 121

electricity, 18, 39, 84–85, 87, 139

Ethiopia, 53, 87

European Union, 26, 29, 60–62, 85, 87, 110, 145, 150, 153

extinction and species loss, 26, 33, 40, 56, 59

F

Fiji, 27, 115

floods, 21, 25–26, 44–45, 47–48, 56, 59, 80–81, 102–105, 111, 113, 120–121, 128

foreign investment laws, 37–42

fossil fuels, 30, 37–39, 42, 58, 62, 75–76, 78–81, 84–86, 119, 121, 153

France, 112

free market ideologies, 67–74, 90–92, 96

G

Gambia, 27

Germany, 85

Glasgow Dialogue, 23

Global Deal for Nature, 32–35

Global Shield Against Climate Risks, 23

greenhouse gases, 18, 20–22, 25–26, 28–29, 32, 35, 38–39, 56–58, 60, 62, 65, 67, 80, 82, 85, 87, 97, 109, 121, 144

greenwashing, 135–163

H

health and a healthy environment, 14–15, 18, 35, 43–45, 47, 50–53, 94–95, 107–109, 112–113, 120–121, 123–125, 128, 141, 144, 151, 165, 169

heat waves, 21, 25–26, 28, 59, 109

human rights, 14–15, 19, 38, 50–54, 103, 126

hurricanes and cyclones, 26–28, 103, 105, 115

I

India, 29, 47, 57, 60, 77, 110

Indigenous peoples, 45, 53–54, 111, 120–121, 123, 125–126

Indonesia, 161

Intergovernmental Panel on Climate Change (IPCC), 40–41, 44, 58–59, 144

Iran, 53, 57

Iraq, 121

J

Japan, 29, 60, 76, 85–87

K

Kenya, 54, 87, 104

Kyoto Protocol, 55–57, 60

Kyrgyzstan, 53

L

lawsuits and legal action, 15, 28, 41–42, 67, 81–83, 130

Lebanon, 121

Libya, 57

"loss and damage," 18, 20–24, 26–28, 30–31, 78, 102, 114–118, 120

M

Malawi, 87, 105–106
Mali, 87
Mexico, 33, 53
Middle East North Africa (MENA), 102, 119, 121
minority groups and issues, 15, 45, 111, 120, 123, 125, 130
Montreal Protocol, 56
Morocco, 121
Mozambique, 47, 87

N

natural and weather disasters, 15, 21–23, 26–28, 30, 34, 43–45, 67, 79, 83, 88, 104, 111, 119, 121, 125, 127–129, 131
natural gas, 39, 58, 61, 85–87, 121, 154–157, 161
Nigeria, 89

O

oil, 15, 39, 58, 61, 67, 74–76, 78–83, 86, 121–122, 154–157, 161

P

Pakistan, 21, 75, 105, 115
Paraguay, 54
Paris Agreement, 32, 35, 40, 52, 55–57, 60–62, 88–89
pollution, 28, 39–40, 51–52, 62–63, 75, 77, 95, 122, 153, 155–156, 161
poverty, 27, 42–49, 74, 86, 102, 107–108, 110–112, 121

R

rainfall, 21, 49, 125
renewable energy and resources, 18, 28, 37–40, 42, 62, 84, 86–87, 130–131, 139, 141, 156
reparations, 15, 18, 22–23, 26
Russia, 29, 53, 85, 87

S

Santiago Network for Loss and Damage, 23, 30–31
Saudi Arabia, 61
Scotland, 23, 30, 85, 103
sea levels, 27, 56, 59, 80, 109, 116, 120
seawalls, 22, 81
Supreme Court, U.S., 79–83
Syria, 53

T

Tonga, 118

Tuvalu, 31

U

Uganda, 87

United Arab Emirates, 56, 61

United Kingdom, 60, 63, 85–88, 145, 153

United Nations (UN), 14, 19–22, 30, 38, 40, 45, 50–54, 56–57, 60, 85–86, 88, 104, 106, 113, 122, 131

United States, 23, 26, 29–30, 56–58, 60–63, 79–83, 85–88, 91, 104, 110

W

water, 14, 21, 27, 32, 39, 49, 51–53, 80, 102–106, 109–111, 116–117, 119–121, 124, 139

women and gender issues, 15, 43–44, 46, 102, 111, 117, 120–121, 123–131

World Bank, 60, 86, 105, 108, 110

World Weather Attribution initiative, 28, 30

Z

Zambia, 105

Y

Yemen, 57